The
FLAVOURS
of
VICTORIA

The FLAVOURS *of* VICTORIA

Andrea & David Spalding

ORCA BOOK PUBLISHERS

First edition.

CANADIAN CATALOGUING IN PUBLICATION DATA
   Spalding, Andrea.
   The flavours of Victoria

   Includes index.
   ISBN 1-55143-014-2

   1. Cookery, Canadian—British Columbia style.   2. Cookery—British Columbia—Victoria.   I. Spalding, David A.E., 1937-   II. Title.
TX715.6.S62 1994   641.59711'2   C94-910156-7

Book design by Arifin Graham, Alaris Design
Cover photo by INFocus Photographic Services/Jeff Barber
Interior colour photographs by Kevin Oke Photography
Archival photographs used with the permission of Victoria City Archives

Printed and bound in Canada

Orca Book Publishers
PO Box 5626, Station B
Victoria, BC
V8R 6S4

*To G and Vin, who have never lost their delight
in creating with food, even in their senior years.*

ACKNOWLEDGEMENTS

Our thanks to the staff of the Victoria Public Library, the Victoria City Archives and the British Columbia Archives and Records Service, and the interpretive staff of Point Ellice House and the Richard Carr House. For specific assistance we gratefully acknowledge the assistance of:

- John Bell, executive officer on HMCS *Yukon*, Esquimalt
- Lee Chan
- Shirley Cukbetson
- Karen Drephal
- Galloping Moon Gallery, Pender Island
- Anne Hennessy, Sutil Lodge, Galiano Island
- Helena and Robert Labbé
- Mike LaCasse, *HMCS Yukon*
- Malcolm Libby
- Stuart Libby
- Georgina Montgomery
- Kevin and Cheryl Oke
- Carey Pallister, Victoria City Archives
- Penny Spalding
- Leslie Stonebridge
- Harriet and Roger Stribley
- Michael Walker, Oak Bay Beach Hotel
- Karon Wallace
- Linda Wolfe

Special thanks are due to Bob Tyrrell, Susan Adamson and Christine Toller of Orca Books, for their interest and enthusiasm.

Contents

Introduction

Victoria is deceptive. Touted for years as a "little bit of Old England" by the tourist department, the British facade seems at first glance to be all encompassing, but it is only a facade. Peer in the cracks and you find not only the long arm of the British Empire, but other equally strong influences that have melded and shaped this town in a uniquely West Coast Canadian way. Among them is food.

Food brought the First Nations here, for the shores were lush, a great green forest punctuated with occasional grassy areas, and edged by rocky bays and beaches. Mink, otter, cougar, deer and bear roamed freely on the land, while the ocean offered everything from minute crustaceans to salmon to whales. Eagles and Turkey Vultures hungrily soared above it all.

Food has been pivotal to almost every happening. The First Nations called one bay Camosack or Camosun — the place for gathering the camas lily, whose starchy bulb was a prized item in their diet. We call the same place Victoria, after an English queen who never set foot on these shores, but whose Hudson's Bay Company needed a safe self-supporting haven to enable it to ship the land's riches back to Britain.

Food has always featured prominently in Victoria. The First Nations fought over the camas bulbs, the British almost fought the Americans over a pig. Food grown here has supplied everyone from settlers in the area, the British Navy and currently the Canadian Navy, and was shipped to early outposts up the coast, to Hawaii and to the Russians in Alaska. Feeding hungry goldminers brought prosperity to some early settlers with business acumen, and feeding thousands of today's tourists accounts for much of Victoria's current prosperity.

So come with us and take a not-too-serious look at Victoria through food. We've discovered some recipes that were new to us and met some old ones in different contexts. We found references to familiar recipes and others we've adapted from historical notes. Rediscover the many aspects of a beautiful city through a different slant — a city that came into being through great natural abundance, yet developed through dynamic foreign influence, a trend that still continues. "We are what we eat" has never been truer than in Victoria, and the resulting "stew" is rich and tasty and leaves one coming back for more.

Andrea and David Spalding

NOTES

For the purpose of this book, Victoria refers to the Greater Victoria area and includes adjacent municipalities such as Esquimalt and Oak Bay.

This book is written using the common Canadian household measurements, which have never really changed in the kitchen despite metrication. All temperatures are Fahrenheit.

Abbreviations

lb = pound	qt = quart
oz = ounce	Tbsp = tablespoon
pkg = package	tsp = teaspoon

For those of you who use metric or British cooking standards, the following information might be useful.

Liquid Measures

1 English pint = 2 cups   1 litre = 4 cups

Solid Measures

2 lbs 2 ozs = 1 kilogram   1 lb fat = 2 cups
1 lb flour = 4 cups

As all recipes don't easily convert, if you are visiting from another country we recommend you pick up a cheap set of Canadian plastic measuring cups and spoons at the supermarket. These will give you the best results.

Oven Temperatures

Temperatures are in Fahrenheit. For the convenience of visitors from other countries, we have added Celsius and Gas Mark equivalents.

Fahrenheit (°F)	Celsius (°C)	Gas Mark
150	70	
175	80	
200	100	
225	110	1/4
250	120	1/2
275	140	1
300	150	2
325	160	3
350	180	4
375	190	5
400	200	6
425	220	7
450	230	8
475 – 525	240 – 275	9

1

In the Beginning

I n the beginning, the natural world offered everything the First Peoples needed. The cedar trees provided the boards for their beautiful large airy houses and their hollowed trunks made canoes, for fishing and whaling. Stripped cedar bark was not only woven into clothing, but also into baskets used for gathering and storing the abundant food found in the forest, shore and ocean.

Food was stored on high shelves in the long houses, where the air could circulate around it and keep it fresh — a method perfect for storing dried clams and berries. The great drying racks for salmon ran from beam to beam. Storage holes were dug in the floor for foods that needed darkness and an even temperature. And some of the bent cedar boxes also contained food.

This land of plenty meant the people didn't have to expend all their energy on food gathering. They had time to tell stories, decorate household objects and clothing, and dance, drum and sing. The culture became strong and vibrant and the ceremonial feast became an important part of life.

Many years ago, we were lucky enough to attend a feast given by the B.C. Provincial Museum (now the Royal B.C. Museum) in the Mungo Martin long house in Thunderbird Park. We will never forget the sights, smells and tastes. The long house interior with the firelight flickering on the wall, the faint hint of smoke and the aroma of the salmon cooking, the lingering flavour of oolichan, the crunch of toasted seaweed, the delicate taste of limpets, barnacles and clams baked in their shells, and the hot bannock and fresh berries. Then the dances started. The masks came to life and the house was peopled with the spirits of the deep woods and the sea. That night lives on in our memories and instilled in us a deep regard for the Native culture and a taste for the natural fruits of the sea and land, some of which have become a part of our diet.

Here are some simple recipes based on early West Coast food and preparation techniques.

BANNOCK

A quick and easy unleavened bread adopted by First Nations people across Canada, bannock can be cooked in the oven, in a frying pan over a campfire or even wrapped around a peeled stick and toasted over hot coals. Children love it hot for breakfast with a little honey drizzled over the top. We sometimes oil the top and sprinkle it with sesame seeds.
Serves 4.

3 cups flour
3 tsp baking powder
1 tsp sea salt
1 to 1½ cups water

- Sift dry ingredients together.
- Add water and combine quickly and lightly with a fork. Knead lightly the last few seconds.

Oven Cooked
- Spread in a greased pie plate and bake at 400° for approximately 20 minutes.
- Cut into wedges and serve.

Pan Fried
- Spread in a greased frying pan, cover and cook until light brown and crisp (not burnt) on the bottom.
- Flip and cook uncovered until done.
- Cut into wedges and serve.

Campfire
- Peel a long green stick; wrap a small handful of dough around the end.
- Hold over the fire and keep turning until cooked.
- Pull off the stick and poke some jam in the middle.
- Serve hot.

⌒

Fruits of the Forest

The forests abound with shoots, roots and leaves that make wonderful salads. In the spring the Coast Salish people who lived in this area delighted in finding such delicacies as the first horsetail shoots and the first sprouts of the Salmon Berry. It's thought that the open space that attracted the Hudson's Bay to the inner harbour was made by the women rolling back turf and digging up the camas lily bulbs with sharp sticks.

WILD SALAD

Those of us brought up with vegetable gardens find the concept of foraging in the forest a little unnerving. So here is a selection of well-known and easily identified wild greens that make a great salad. You can also just add one or two of these ingredients to a garden salad for little pizzas.
Serves 4.

2 cups young fresh dandelion leaves
¼ cup wild beach mustard leaves
½ cup sorrel
1 cup wild onions, bulb and tops, chopped
¼ cup sea asparagus, chopped

- Wash, dry and tear the dandelion and sorrel leaves.
- Wash, dry and cut in half the wild beach mustard leaves.
- Toss together with chopped wild onion.
- Add a light dressing *(see suggestion below).*
- Toss again and sprinkle the chopped sea asparagus over the top.

Salad Dressing
Because wild salad ingredients taste stronger than our garden lettuce, we like to use a light dressing with a hint of fruit. Use a fruit flavoured vinegar like blackberry vinegar, or a red wine vinegar with a light oil recipe *(see page 155).*

> ### ROYAL B.C. MUSEUM
>
> *The Royal B.C. Museum on Belleville Street has some wonderful exhibits on the First Peoples, including a long house and exhibits featuring food and preparation and storage techniques. The museum is open daily and well worth the price of admission. Allow plenty of time; there's lots to see.*

People of the Salmon

The Coastal people are the people of the salmon. Salmon was the staple food, and it was cooked and preserved in many different ways. Their way of life is centred around the life cycle and seasons of the salmon, and the salmon features in many of their ceremonies, stories, songs and art.

SALMON LOX ON BANNOCK

One of the quickest hors d'oeuvres we know.
Makes 8 wedges.

1 recipe fresh baked bannock *(see page 2)*
4 ozs lox, thinly sliced
¼ cup salmon roe
¼ cup wild onion, chopped

- Make bannock and bake according to recipe.
- Cut in wedges, lay salmon slices on top and sprinkle with roe and chopped onion.
- Broil for a few seconds until edges of salmon crisp and some of the roe pops.
- Serve immediately as an hors d'oeuvre.

Smoking Fish

First Nations people made smokehouses for their fish, something that many West Coast people do today. In fact, small smokehouse kits can be purchased at several hardware and sportfishing stores in Victoria.

SMOKED SALMON SOUP

Serves 6.

1 lb smoked salmon
6 cups water
salt and pepper, to taste
1 cup watercress, chopped
1 cup wild or green onions, chopped

- Bring water to boil, turn down heat until just simmering.
- Break up salmon into small pieces, drop into water. Add salt and pepper to taste.
- Simmer gently for 10 minutes, stirring occasionally.
- Add chopped watercress and onions.
- Stir gently, simmer a further 5 minutes.

POACHED SALMON

Though this is based on a traditional recipe, it is healthily modern in its simplicity.
Serves 6.

6 – ½ inch-thick salmon steaks

Poaching broth
12 large field mushrooms, sliced
½ cup watercress, chopped
6 wild or green onions with tops
1 tsp sea salt
½ tsp black pepper
4 cups chicken bouillon, fresh or canned

- Heat chicken bouillon, add watercress, sliced mushrooms, whole onions and seasonings. Simmer gently for 10 minutes.
- Cool to room temperature.
- Place salmon steaks in frying pan. Cover with broth and poach gently for 15 minutes.
- Serve with steamed sorrel or spinach with the broth sprinkled over.

THUNDERBIRD PARK

Situated beside the Royal B.C. Museum, Thunderbird Park has a spectacular collection of totems and house posts. There is also a carving shed that is often open to the public so you can see work in progress. Several totem poles can also be seen in other parts of Victoria, including Beacon Hill Park. The salmon image is often used; see if you can pick it out.

A World Before Briquettes

The First Nations invented the barbecue method of cooking. Before metal grills were available, the salmon was pinned to a board that was propped over hot coals so the salmon could broil. Sorrel was crushed and the juice gathered and this was dripped over the salmon as seasoning.

GRILLED SALMON

Serves 6.

6 – 1½ inch-thick salmon steaks
6 wild or green onions
    or 6 garlic cloves
sea salt and pepper, to taste

- Prepare barbecue with coals hot and glowing.
- Lay steaks in grill and cover with onions or crushed garlic.
- Grill 3 to 4 minutes a side about 5 inches from the coals.
- Season with salt and pepper.

Fungus Forays

Foraging for roots, berries and mushrooms was women's work, and the fall fungus season was enjoyed as fungus collecting was less arduous than some other harvesting tasks. The fungi were collected in the large woven baskets, some were air-dried and others eaten fresh. The following recipe is good made with the common field mushrooms, but also delicious made with slices of puffball.

Steamed mussels, Bannock (baked), Wild salad

Seaweed being dried on the Saanichton Reserve about 1937

BREAKFAST MUSHROOMS

The large field mushrooms are still found in some of the wilder areas of Victoria parks. Don't collect them, though, unless you know for sure what species they are. Many grocery stores also carry them in the fall mushroom season.
Serves 2.

8 large black field mushrooms, sliced
1 tsp butter
salt and pepper
3 Tbsp red wine

• Cook all ingredients in pan till wine has reduced to a sauce.
• Serve on hot buttered toast.

Early Beach Parties

While salmon was a staple item, the Coast Salish diet was varied and healthy. Clams, mussels and limpets were gathered, and dried, baked or steamed. (Clambakes were not a Hollywood movie invention.) The fat and juicy oysters were enjoyed cooked or raw.

MIDDENS

Many beaches are headed by a large ridge of shells, sometimes many feet high. This shows that you are on an early gathering ground. These middens have been formed over thousands of years of First Nations people harvesting and eating clams, sea urchins, mussels and oysters and discarding the shells in a heap at the head of the beach. Sometimes artifacts such as scrapers and harpoons or carved spoons are found in the middens, but usually all you can see are the layers of shells interspersed with layers of ashes from the fires where the food was cooked. Middens can be seen on almost all low bank beaches where the transition between land and beach has not been altered, usually park areas or natural coves on the Saanich Peninsula and in Sooke.

SAUTÉED OYSTERS

There are two species of oysters found in these waters, but use the Giant Pacific Oysters for a real treat.
Serves 2 as a main dish, 4 as hors d'oeuvres.

12 large shucked oysters, rinsed
3 garlic cloves, crushed
2 tsp butter or vegetable oil
4 wild or green onions with tops, chopped

- Heat butter or oil in frying pan.
- Add garlic and onions and sauté until transparent.
- Add oysters and cook gently until they change colour.
- Turn oysters and cook till just firm but not rubbery.
- Serve with hot fresh bread or bannock.

STEAMED MUSSELS OR CLAMS

Often served in restaurants as an appetizer, when served in a large bowl accompanied by lots of fresh French bread (or bannock) to mop up the broth, this is a complete meal.
Serves 4 as an appetizer or 2 as a main dish.

4 doz fresh mussels or clams
2 cups white wine
2 garlic cloves, chopped
2 green onions, including stems, chopped
1 large tomato, quartered
1 celery stalk, chopped in 2 inch pieces

- Rinse and scrub mussels.
- Place all ingredients in a wok and bring to the boil.
- Cover with lid and steam until mussels open (approximately 5 minutes).
- Discard any mussels that have not opened.
- Ladle mussels into dishes and share out the broth. Serve immediately with small forks for picking out the meat.

NOTE: *When storing fresh mussels before cooking, they should be in an uncovered bowl in the fridge. Do not cover or they will suffocate and die. As they also smell fishy, place the bowl near the baking soda.*

ROASTED GOOSE

Many kinds of wild game were hunted by the Coast Salish and enjoyed roasted over the fire. This cooking method was also used by the early fort personnel and settlers, who roasted game on spits over open fires. Oven roasting makes meat almost as tasty today and is a whole lot easier, but we do admit that the flavour is better if game is roasted on a carefully tended spit over the barbecue. The recipe below is a First Nations adaptation of traditional and non-traditional ingredients. The stuffing is also delicious with turkey.

Serves 10 to 12 people.

2 Canada geese (approximately 6 lbs each)
   or 1 domestic goose (10 to 12 lbs)

Stuffing
12 wild or green onions
4 cups dried crumbled bannock or breadcrumbs
6 celery stalks
2 cups fresh cranberries
½ lb mushrooms
1 lb dried prunes, boiled (save juice)
1 Tbsp salt
½ tsp black pepper
1 tsp savory or thyme
2 cups rye whisky
giblets
1 qt water

- Simmer giblets in water for 30 minutes.
- Drain and cool liquid, skim off fat.
- Chop giblet meat.
- Rinse geese and pat dry.
- Chop onions, celery, cranberries, mushrooms and prunes.
- Mix all chopped ingredients with the giblets and the bannock crumbs.
- Combine rye and prune juice.
- Moisten stuffing with ½ cup of rye mixture and enough giblet water to hold together.
- Stuff into the body cavity of the geese and the neck area. Pull skin carefully over it, and sew.
- Prick skin all over goose, and place on a wire rack in a roasting pan.
- Roast uncovered at 350° for approximately 4 hours, basting frequently with the remaining rye mixture.

SAUCE FOR THE GOOSE
(GREEN GOOSEBERRY SAUCE)

If goose is served in summer when the gooseberries are ripe, green gooseberry sauce makes a great accompaniment. The acidity counteracts the grease from the bird.

1⅔ cups fresh gooseberries
1 lemon, grated rind and juice of
1 Tbsp butter, melted
1 tsp sugar
salt and pepper, to taste

- Top and tail gooseberries and place in saucepan with the lemon juice and rind. Cover and shake gently over low heat until fruit is tender.
- Place in food processor and make purée.
- While running pour in melted butter and sugar.
- Season with salt and pepper.
- Pour into warmed sauce boat and serve.

Songhees Point

A group of Coast Salish known as the Songhees lived in the Cadboro Bay area, but moved to the Inner Harbour area in 1858, attracted by the activity of the growing settlement. This was not a popular move as far as the settlement's population was concerned. Curiosity turned to distrust, mainly due to lack of understanding of the Native culture. The staff of the Saunders Grocery store were offended by the Songhees women sitting on the storefront window ledge, so installed a row of spikes. Others were upset at the Songhees for sitting on the sidewalk and selling potatoes, clams and salmon. Eventually the Songhees were moved to Esquimalt. It took until the present decade for their place in the tapestry of Victoria to be publicly accepted. They are remembered in the name of Songhees Peninsula, and the shore walk starting at Ocean Pointe is now dedicated to the Native population that once lived there.

2

Fort Victoria

In 1942 Hudson's Bay factor James Douglas was touring the coast of southern Vancouver Island looking for a suitable site for a new Hudson's Bay fort and trading post. After a lot of deliberating he chose a place on the southern tip of Vancouver Island, a place the Native people called Camosack (Camosun). Of course the local inhabitants were not asked if they wished to have British traders in their front yard, and there are conflicting reports as to their reaction. One historian reports that the Songhees welcomed the building of the fort and helped cut the cedar pickets, but another refers to a "flurry" with the Indians. Whatever the original reaction, the fields of camas lilies lost. The site Douglas chose is now close to Victoria's Inner Harbour. It was within twenty yards of the ocean and surrounded by a fertile plain suitable not only for building, but for agriculture.

Construction of a small fort – one hundred yards square – began in March 1843, but in 1846 the Oregon Boundary Treaty was signed and the British were forced to move north of the 49th parallel. This made tiny Fort Victoria the chief western outpost of the British Empire, and politically, it gained in stature. It even grew a little in size as Douglas's assessment of the fertile land proved true. In 1847, 300 acres produced 1000 bushels of wheat, 400 of peas, 700 of oats and 3000 of potatoes, and the farm had a commodious cowhouse! By 1849 Britain declared that Vancouver Island was officially a Crown Colony, under the protection of the Hudson's Bay Company. This sounded very important, but actually not much changed, and only a few settlers came. In fact, it took the discovery of gold to put Victoria on the map. All that remains of the fort is seen in and around Bastion Square. Watch for an outline of the fort marked in bricks sunk into the sidewalk. The name Fort Street, now marking a busy traffic artery, was once attached to a pastoral trail winding from the fort through the surrounding countryside.

Compared with other Hudson's Bay forts across the country, life at Fort Victoria was very pleasant. The weather was temperate, and the land and ocean bountiful. The home-grown vegetables and a small collection of pigs and cattle were added to the abundance of seafood, wild game, herbs and berries. Trading for local delicacies with the Songhees added even more variety. In Fort Victoria they ate well.

Here are some historic recipes that might well have been served on a regular basis in the fort, several of which are still enjoyed today.

BAKED BEANS

Beans were the backbone of early Canada, an easily transportable, long-lasting dried product that, when cooked, turned into a high-protein, stick-to-the-ribs, comforting and energizing dish. Beans were the grand old staple of the Canadian fur traders, explorers, settlers, sailors, mounties and Klondikers and are still regularly eaten today (though often from a can). The secret to a good pot of beans has never changed – long, slow cooking.
    Serves 6.

2 cups navy beans
8 cups water

Night Before
• Wash beans well in running water and place in a large pot.
• Add the water and soak overnight.

Next Day
• Drain beans, place in large pot and cover with water.
• Bring to the boil and boil rapidly for 1 to 2 minutes, skimming off any white frothy scum.
• Reduce heat and simmer very gently, uncovered, for approximately 1 hour, until the skins split when blown upon.
• Drain and place in a bean crock.
• Preheat oven to 250°.

1 large onion, cut into eighths
½ lb salt pork, diced

⅓ cup brown sugar
1 Tbsp salt
1½ tsp dry mustard
½ tsp black pepper
½ cup fancy molasses
boiling water

- Stir the onions and diced pork into the beans.
- Mix together all the other ingredients except water and pour over the beans.
- Add enough boiling water to cover the beans.
- Cover crock and bake in 250° oven for 8 hours.
- Check occasionally and add a little boiling water so that the beans do not become dry.
- Uncover for the last 30 minutes.
- Serve with hot fresh porridge bread.

PORRIDGE BREAD

Many Hudson's Bay personnel, including Douglas, were of Scottish ancestry, so oats were another staple item found in the fort. Now known as oatmeal bread, this recipe is still popular.

Makes 3 loaves.

1 cup rolled oats
2 tsp salt
3 Tbsp butter
2 cups boiling water
1 tsp sugar
½ cup lukewarm water
1 pkg active dry yeast
½ cup molasses
1 cup wheat flour
4 to 5 cups all-purpose flour

- In a large bowl combine the first three ingredients and pour the boiling water over them.
- Stir until the butter melts; cool to lukewarm.
- In a small bowl, dissolve the sugar in the lukewarm water and sprinkle the dried yeast over it. Let stand for 10 minutes. Stir briskly with a fork.

- Mix the yeast mixture into the rolled oat mixture along with the molasses.
- Sift the wheat and white flour together.
- Using the dough hook on a mixer, beat flour into the oat mixture, 1 cup at a time. If the last cup won't absorb, turn the dough out onto a board and knead it in by hand.
- Continue kneading for 8 to 10 minutes.
- Grease a large warm bowl. Place dough in bowl, turning so all surfaces get greased.
- Cover and let rise until doubled in size (1½ to 2 hours).
- Punch down, divide and shape into 3 loaves.
- Place in greased loaf pans, grease tops of loaves, cover and let rise until doubled.
- Bake in a preheated oven at 375° for 1 hour.

Meat and Salt

Without refrigeration, the only way to keep meat was by drying or salting. The salting method left the meat almost inedible to today's palates. Cooking in milk was a standard method used to reduce the saltiness of meat. Here is an original recipe followed by a modern adaptation.

FRIED SALT PORK

Salt pork can still be purchased, though it's usually only bought in small quantities for dishes like the baked bean recipe.

- Cut as many slices of salt pork as needed.
- Put in half milk and half water to cover; sweet or sour milk can be used.
- Let soak 6 hours.
- Rinse till the water is clear.
- Fry. It is nearly as nice as fresh pork.
- Can be rolled in corn meal or flour if desired.

HAM BAKED IN MILK

This modern adaptation has stayed around as it makes even our precooked ham very tender and suits our less salty diet.
Serves 4.

2 – 1 inch-thick slices of precooked ham
1 tsp dry mustard
3 Tbsp brown sugar
2 cups milk (approximately)
6 whole cloves
2 bay leaves

- Trim ham slices of all excess fat and fit in a shallow casserole dish.
- Mix the mustard and brown sugar together, and sprinkle over the ham.
- Pour in the milk until it just covers the ham.
- Add the cloves and bay leaves.
- Cover and bake in a preheated oven, 30 minutes at 300°.

The Game's the Thing

Freshly caught wild game and fish were regular items and a welcome change from beans and salt meat. While large-game hunting was the preserve of men, squirrels were plentiful and were often caught by the children, just like the prairie children hunted gophers. They were delicious, and an anonymous visitor noted, "Supped on squirrel stew, tender and flavoursome." (Nowadays squirrels are less common around the city, and we shouldn't be tempted.) There are no native rabbits on Vancouver Island, but both European and cottontail rabbits were soon introduced as another food source. Rabbit and squirrel recipes can also be made with chicken.

BUNNY HILL

For those of you who prefer to see a bunny in the field rather than on your plate, wild rabbits can be seen by the dozen on the hill by the new Victoria General Hospital on Helmcken Road. In fact, the rabbits have the run of the hospital grounds, much to the delight of the patients and visitors, many of whom feed them.

DRUNK JUGGED RABBIT

This is a flavoursome way of cooking a regular pioneer stewpot item. Rabbit can still be purchased in the Victoria area.
    Serves 4 to 6.

    2 rabbits, skinned, drawn and quartered
    4 Tbsp flour
    ½ cup butter
    3 cups water
    2 whole onions, peeled and quartered
    2 bay leaves
    4 whole cloves
    1 tsp allspice
    1 Tbsp salt
    1 tsp pepper
    2 cups wild mushrooms, sliced
    1 cup sherry
    1 Tbsp lemon juice
    cornstarch, if needed

- Wash and pat dry rabbit pieces. Roll in flour, shake off the excess.
- Melt butter in frying pan. Fry rabbit until well browned. Do not burn.
- Place rabbit pieces in stewpan.
- Add leftover flour to remaining butter and fry, stirring into a smooth paste.
- Gradually add the 3 cups of water and cook for 10 minutes.
- Pour the liquid over the rabbit.
- Stir in the onions, bay leaves, cloves, allspice, salt, pepper and mushrooms.
- Cover and simmer for 1½ hours.
- Stir in the sherry and the lemon juice (if gravy needs thickening, combine a little cornstarch with the sherry).
- Serve with boiled rice.

CAMP BISCUITS

This recipe was found in the diary of an early settler who noted that it "makes good dumplings, as well as oven biscuits." We make it regularly, substituting margarine for the lard. This goes really well with stews made with wild meats.
    Makes 30 biscuits.

6 cups flour
6 tsp baking powder
½ tsp salt
3 Tbsp lard
2 cups cold water

- Mix dry ingredients.
- Rub in lard.
- Mix in water with a fork (do not use fingers) until a stiff dough.
- Flop onto a floured board and pat down gently to ¾ inch thick.
- Cut out rounds and place on cooked stew for dumplings. Finish cooking stew for 15 to 30 minutes.
- For oven biscuits, place rounds on a baking sheet. Cook in a medium oven until browned (approximately 15 to 20 minutes at 350°).

SQUIRREL POT PIE

Serves 4.

4 squirrels, skinned and cleaned
1 handful of flour
1 qt boiling water
1 large onion, chopped
¼ lemon, sliced
pinch salt and pepper
knob good dripping

- Fry onion in dripping till just coloured, remove with slotted spoon and reserve.
- Cut squirrels into pieces. Flour and brown in dripping.
- Add the onion, boiling water and all other ingredients. Cover closely and stew for 1 hour.
- Make a light biscuit crust *(see Camp Biscuit recipe, page 16)*. Cut in rounds and drop on stew to make dumplings.
- Cover closely and boil 15 minutes or until done.
- Place dumplings around edge of a platter and the squirrel in the middle.
- Thicken gravy and pour over the squirrel.

VICTORIANS AND FOOD: LADY AMELIA DOUGLAS

She was born Amelia Connolly, the daughter of an Irish clerk for the North West Company, and his wife, a Cree chief's daughter. Amelia married James Douglas on April 27, 1828 at Fort St James in what is now northern B.C. She was 16! They married "according to the custom of the country," without a lawyer or clergyman present. This caused a great deal of snubbing and gossip during her life in Victoria despite their marriage being formalized by Church of England rites in 1836. She bore eleven children and also brought up three by her eldest daughter Celia, who died after only a few years of marriage.

Amelia took her role as Douglas's wife very seriously, especially after Douglas was appointed Governor of Vancouver Island and they moved into a house built on the site of what is now the Royal B.C. Museum. Here she hosted open houses, luncheons and constant dinner parties for visitors to the fort and for the officers on the visiting ships in Esquimalt. She spent endless time helping other women in the settlement, including several through childbirth. She was also known for buying ducks, fish and berries from the Songhees, who would paddle to the bottom of her garden in their canoes. The food would then be distributed to the poor. The Songhees would paddle back loaded up with fruits and vegetables from her garden.

It was through Amelia's example that, at Fort Victoria, Douglas was able to demand that Hudson's Bay employees honour their marital commitments, so that liaisons between traders and Indian or Métis women at the fort usually turned out to be permanent relationships.

WEED OR FEED?

Vegetables did not seem to have much importance in early diets, but the new spring growth of what we often consider a noxious weed was an occasional treat. Try this.

- Dig up young dandelion plants before they have bloomed (young plantain and clover are good, too).
- Wash well (particularly where the root and leaves join). Chop.
- Toss with a chopped wild onion.
- Dress with oil and vinegar.

Fishy Dishes

Fish was a daily staple at the fort; sometimes fish dishes appeared at every meal. Favourites included salmon and Lingcod from the sea below the fort, and trout from the streams and lakes further inland. Despite today's more elaborate cooking techniques, some old-timers swear that the only way to cook fresh Rainbow Trout is campfire style.

TRADITIONAL CAMPFIRE TROUT

1 trout per person
salt
bacon grease
corn meal

- Clean trout by slitting the belly with a sharp knife and removing the guts without breaking them.
- Slit neck behind the gills and break off head. This will leave only the air sac and a little blood by the backbone. Scrape away gently with a fingernail, being careful not to break the delicate ribs.
- Rinse and pat dry.
- Heat some bacon grease in a frying pan until hot.
- Salt the body cavity lightly.
- Roll trout in corn meal.
- Fry until trout crisps and sizzles on one side, turn and fry till crisp on the other.
- The trout is cooked when the dark brown skin will break away from the pink meat and the tail curls up to offer you a handle.

Formality at the Fort

Although one imagines simple and frugal meals eaten at the fort, this was not quite true. Factor Douglas insisted on formal dining on a daily basis (at least for the men — the women and children ate separately). The mess room was graced by a large table set with a spotless white linen cloth and a row of sparkling decanters, and surrounded by Windsor chairs brought from England. Douglas regularly gave banquets and celebratory meals where roasts of game would be served with hearty and elaborate side dishes, washed down with gallons of wine and sherry. There were numerous toasts and often the singing lasted far into the night.

ONES THAT MIGHT NOT GET AWAY

Fish are still plentiful in the Victoria area. Although boats are available for hire, many people get their jollies (and their fish) by surf casting from the shore. Spring salmon up to 23 lbs have been caught from Ten Mile Point and the Dallas Road Breakwater. With the right equipment, Lingcod can also be caught on rubber worms. Occasionally, oddities like the Wolf-Eel and octopus are pulled in, and end up in the local aquarium.

If you prefer your water without waves, Rainbow Trout still swim in the Goldstream and Sooke rivers, and several of the nearby lakes are also stocked for recreational fishing. Inquire at tackle shops and marinas about licences and favourite lures. Many locals are into home smoking, but local smokehouse services will preserve your catch so you can take it back home to impress your friends.

FRESH TROUT FRENCH STYLE

For those of us not into bacon grease, here is a modern method, almost as simple, and we think even more delicious.

This recipe is for one person, so adjust accordingly for friends.

1 fresh trout, cleaned
2 lemons, juice of
4 ozs Jamaican rum
salt, to taste
3 lemon slices, for garnish

- Wash whole trout inside and out, and pat dry.
- Salt inside cavity and over skin.
- Place in a shallow dish. Pour lemon juice and rum over fish.
- Cover and leave to marinate for 1 hour.
- Remove from marinade and wrap fish tightly in foil.
- Bake in 500° oven for 30 minutes.
- Unwrap and place on platter. Garnish with lemon slices and serve with tiny new potatoes, tiny new beets and fresh garden peas.

ROAST VENISON

Here is a modern version of a dish Douglas must have sampled many times. If you don't hunt, it's worth cultivating a neighbour who does just to try this out! Delicious.

1 large venison roast
8 slices of bacon
1 cup beef bouillon
1 cup red wine
¼ cup lemon juice
6 large garlic cloves, crushed
1 tsp salt
½ tsp pepper
½ tsp fresh thyme

- Preheat oven to 500°.
- Weigh meat and note poundage.
- Wash, dry and trim all fat off roast.
- Place in roasting pan and sear in oven for 10 minutes.
- Remove and reduce oven heat to 425°.
- Place the bacon slices over the roast.
- Return to oven and roast uncovered for 40 minutes (remove bacon when it's turned brown).
- Combine remaining ingredients. Pour over the roast at the end of the 40-minute period.
- Cover roasting pan loosely with foil, return to oven and start timing again — 20 minutes per pound for medium-rare.
- Baste frequently.

HUNTING

Game hunting is restricted on Vancouver Island, but still high on the official list of recreational activities. Deer and duck hunting are particularly popular (though in some areas only a bow and arrow is permitted). You can obtain a free copy of B.C. Hunting Regulations from sporting goods stores, or from the Ministry of the Environment, Lands and Parks.

FORT STREET

No more a winding wagon trail, Fort Street is now a trail of another kind – the book lovers' and antique hunters' trail. Often called Antique Row, Fort Street boasts antique shop after antique shop, interspersed with secondhand book stores, which make it a bargain hunter's delight. But the trail is long on a hot day, so wear your walking shoes. Luckily, there are some excellent restaurants along the way to allow for rest and recuperation.

TRAIL MIX

Something to snack on when hot on the trail up Antique Row (or almost anywhere else).

- In a large bowl mix together any combination of the following:

  husked sunflower seeds
  peanuts
  almonds
  raisins
  dried apricots, chopped
  dried apples, chopped
  dates, chopped
  Smarties or chocolate chips
  any kind of salted mini-cocktail crackers

- Pour a couple of scoops of the mixture into small ziplock plastic bags. Seal.
- Hand out as individual iron rations when family tempers begin to fray.
- Will keep indefinitely.

EDIBLE LEGACY

There is a Black Prince cherry tree growing on the grounds of the Royal British Columbia Museum that is reputed to have grown from a cherry pit planted in 1854 by James Douglas. The grounds were once part of the Douglas orchard.

Baked beans and Whole-wheat coffee can bread

The official residence of Sir James Douglas – scene of many a high tea – still stood at the turn of the century

3

Gold Rush City

In 1858, with the discovery of gold in the Fraser River, Fort Victoria found itself firmly on the world map. Thousands of miners from the worked-out California gold fields travelled up the west coast towards Vancouver Island. It started quietly enough. One Sunday evening in April 1858, the S.S. *Commodore* anchored in the harbour. There was nothing remarkable about this, until the gangplank was lowered and four hundred and fifty goldminers streamed off, and in July another fifty-five hundred arrived. Victoria became an instant tent city.

VICTORIANS AND FOOD: AMOR DE COSMOS

He arrived in Fort Victoria with the miners. His name was William Smith, a former grocery store assistant from Nova Scotia, but he preferred to be called Amor de Cosmos ("lover of the universe"). Cosmos left a legend and a legacy. His eccentric behaviour and outrageous public battles were legion. (He led the arguments for Vancouver Island to align itself with the States rather than the Canadian Confederation.) He also founded a newspaper called the British Colonist, which survives today as the Times-Colonist. One story tells of the time he was elected to the legislature and he rose and spoke for seven hours non-stop, energy being provided at regular intervals by tumblerfuls of eggnog.

This sudden influx of itinerant males changed the whole ambience of Fort Victoria. Some people hated the rough, tough life the settlement was plunged into, but many local citizens rubbed their hands with glee. Suddenly they had a seemingly insatiable demand for food and services. Several original settlers promptly started outfitting businesses that made their fortune.

THE ULTIMATE EGGNOG

We assume Cosmos fortified himself with homemade eggnog, so we offer you the most incredible eggnog we have ever tasted. We serve it every New Year. It's supposed to feed a large party, but it is so delicious that it disappears like snow in the sun no matter how small the group. It's definitely worth the effort, but its side effect might mean you offer your guests a bed for the night.

1 doz eggs
4 cups heavy cream
4 cups light cream
1¾ cups sugar
26 ozs rye whisky
4 ozs rum
3 ozs cognac
2 tsp ground nutmeg

- Separate eggs into 2 stainless steel or glass bowls (do not use plastic).
- Beat yolks with 1½ cups sugar (reserve the other ¼ cup) until thick and creamy.
- Clean beaters, beat egg whites until thick, beat in reserved ¼ cup sugar and continue beating until whites hold peaks.
- In a large punch bowl, combine yolks and whites by mixing gently on low speed.
- Add the cream, combining gently.
- Stir in the rye, rum and cognac.
- Sprinkle nutmeg on top.
- Let sit in the fridge for at least 1 hour. A foamy crust will form.
- Serve in glasses, making sure some liquid and foam are in each glass.

Food for the Miners

The men heading for the gold fields became known as "Sourdoughs" because they carried sourdough starter in bags tucked inside their shirts to keep it warm. This starter was used to make a quick-rising bread that could be cooked over the campfire.

Sourdough bread is still a Western Canadian favourite, and sourdough loaves can be found in several Victoria bakeries.

GOLD RUSH SOURDOUGH BISCUITS

This original sourdough recipe can be cooked in a frying pan if you want to be really authentic, but the biscuits are even lighter and more delicious when cooked on a baking sheet in the oven.
Makes 12 biscuits.

1 cup live sourdough starter
1 cup all-purpose flour
¼ tsp baking soda
2 tsp baking powder
¼ cup margarine

- Mix flour, baking soda and baking powder together in a bowl.
- Rub or cut in the margarine until the mixture is the texture of small breadcrumbs.
- Add the culture and mix with a fork until almost combined. Finish kneading with hands until smooth (about 10 times).
- Spread a lightly floured tea cloth on the counter and place sourdough in the middle.
- Gently pat the dough flat until it's about a ½ inch thick. Cut out biscuits with a floured cutter.
- Place on a baking sheet and for best results let stand at room temperature for 30 minutes.
- Bake in oven preheated to 350° for 15 to 20 minutes.

To cook in a frying pan
- Grease a heavy iron frying pan well. Place biscuits about a ½ inch apart. Cover and cook on medium heat for 10 minutes a side.
- Serve hot with butter.

NOTE: *These freeze well.*

FEEDING SOURDOUGH STARTER

1 cup flour
1 cup milk
1/4 cup sugar

- Always leave at least 1 cup of your original sourdough starter in a clean screw-top jar.
- Add the above ingredients to the starter and stir well.
- Cover the jar and place in the fridge.
- Allow a rest period of 24 hours after feeding before using again.
- Divide culture regularly to keep it active. The instructions always say use once a week, but we can keep ours up to three weeks without killing it.

RISING TO THE OCCASION

If you cannot find a friend who will rise to the occasion and share some live starter with you, a packet of dried starter can be bought from several specialty kitchen stores in Victoria. We've also seen it in the gift shop at Craigdarroch Castle. The instructions are included.

FLAPJACKS

Flapjacks, or pancakes, were another gold rush staple. Quick and easy to make, flapjacks provided early-morning energy for the arduous trip to the gold fields.
Makes enough for 4 medium or 2 hearty appetites.

1 1/2 cups all-purpose flour
3 tsp baking powder
1/4 tsp salt
1 Tbsp sugar
1 egg
1 3/4 cups milk
2 Tbsp melted shortening or vegetable oil

- Sift together the dry ingredients in one bowl.
- Beat together the liquid and egg in another bowl.
- Combine the dry ingredients with the wet and stir until almost smooth.
- Grease a heavy frying pan, preheat and pour in about 1/4 cup of batter per pancake.
- Turn when bubbles break the surface.
- Serve hot with butter and maple syrup.

Modern Variants
- Stir some fresh blueberries into the batter (½ to ¾ cup).
- Stir in ¾ cup grated apple and a pinch of nutmeg.

BOILED DINNER

When travelling to the Gold Rush, you travelled as light as possible – at least, as light as you could when packing in a year's supply of food. One-pot meals were the order of the day. This often resulted in the inevitable boiled dinner, a dish also favoured by pioneer women struggling with children, washing, milking and the hundred other chores that left little time for fancy cooking. It's actually a lot tastier that it sounds, partially due to the spices in the corned beef. The current equivalent would be pot roast.

4 to 5 lbs corned beef
6 carrots
6 medium onions
2 turnips
2 parsnips
6 potatoes
1 small cabbage head
salt and pepper, to taste

- Place the meat in a large kettle, cover with water and bring to the boil.
- Cover, reduce heat and simmer for 3 to 4 hours or until tender.
- Quarter all the small vegetables and cut the cabbage in wedges.
- An hour before the meat is fully cooked, skim off any fat and add the carrots, onions, turnips and parsnips.
- Cook for a further 30 minutes, add the potatoes and cabbage.
- Check seasoning and cook till tender.
- Place the meat on a large platter and arrange the vegetables around it.
- Serve the gravy separately.

VEGETABLE HASH

There were usually leftovers from a large pot of boiled dinner. These were used the next morning.

- Coarsely chop any vegetables left over from last night's boiled dinner, such as cabbage, parsnips, potatoes.
- Sprinkle well with salt and pepper.
- Melt a knob of butter in a frying pan, turning the pan so the sides and bottom are coated.
- Put in the chopped vegetables.
- Pour in a spoonful or two of hot water from the tea kettle and cover quickly to keep in the steam.
- Stir occasionally until well cooked.
- Serve hot.

Hash Updated

Vegetable hash becomes a delicious modern breakfast hash when gingered up as follows.

- Sauté a chopped onion and chopped garlic clove in the butter before adding the rest of the vegetables.
- Add some chopped fresh dill and a little red pepper sauce.

VICTORIANS AND FOOD: THOMAS HARRIS

Arriving in town as a miner, Harris sized up Victoria and decided there was more money to be made as a merchant, so he opened the first butcher shop. His store, Queen's Market, became one of the most popular butcher stores in Victoria, partially because of the colourful character of its owner, and definitely for the prices. For instance, prime rib roast was 15 cents per pound, but with liver, kidney and spare ribs thrown in – he didn't charge for offal.

Harris definitely lived up to the maxim "you are what you eat." By the time he was elected mayor of Victoria he weighed three hundred pounds. Once, while presiding over a council meeting in the fort, he leaned back in his chair. There was a splintering sound and he disappeared from view, landing on "that portion of his breeches that wears out first." The British Colonist reported "the crash was so loud that it set the doors and windows to rattling loudly," while the remains of the chair looked like "a crushed eggshell."

POTATO SOUP

Soup was another popular item found in Tent City, particularly when the ingredients were hearty and cheap.

Serves 6.

4 medium potatoes
1½ cups beef stock
1½ cups water
1 tsp salt
16 ozs evaporated milk
1 small green onion, stem included, chopped
3 Tbsp butter
pepper, to taste
½ cup grated cheese
handful parsley, chopped

- Peel and quarter potatoes; boil in the beef stock and water with salt.
- Drain, reserving liquid. Press potatoes through a sieve.
- Combine potato liquid with the evaporated milk.
- Stir in the chopped onion and butter, and add pepper to taste.
- Heat but do not boil.
- Stir in the sieved potatoes. Reheat carefully, but do not boil.
- Check seasoning then stir in cheese, stirring until melted.
- Serve garnished with parsley.

JOHNNY CAKE

Johnny Cake, thought to be a corruption of Journey cake, was whipped up by miners, settlers and fur traders alike. Made with Indian corn meal, the flavour was a nice change from wheat bread. There are many recipes for Johnny Cake in use today, but we were intrigued by this original one in rhyme.

2 cups Indian, 1 cup wheat
1 cup sour milk, 1 cup sweet,
1 cup good eggs that you can eat,
½ cup molasses too,
½ cup sugar, add thereto,
Salt and soda, each 1 spoon,
Mix up quickly and bake it soon.

- It works. Pour in a greased 8 by 12 inch pan, and bake at 300°
  for 20 minutes, or until centre springs back when touched.

~

The Offal Truth

No one turned up their noses at offal as is so often the case today, especially when the price was right. In the early days the free ribs were often used for dog food, but nowadays we find them a tasty and nutritious source of meat. Another cheap ingredient was cabbage. So many were grown at the fort that some were turned into barrels of sauerkraut, a nutritious staple that added flavour to what was often a bland diet.

BAKED SPARERIBS AND SAUERKRAUT

Serves 4.

4 lbs spareribs
3 lbs sauerkraut

- Preheat oven to 350°.
- Place spareribs in a roasting pan and roast for 30 minutes.
- Remove pan from oven, lift out spareribs. Arrange the sauerkraut in the dripping in the bottom of the pan.
- Turn the spareribs over and place on top of the sauerkraut.
- Bake for 1½ hours.
- Serve with mashed potatoes.

Modern Update
We add chopped garlic and 2 teaspoons caraway seeds to the 'kraut, and sprinkle garlic salt and black pepper on the spareribs. We also check several times while cooking and, if the sauerkraut looks dry, add a little water or white wine and cover loosely with foil.

~

Ruckus with Rice

Not all the miners were poor. Some had money to fling around, and bars and clubs quickly sprang up to meet the demand. Victoria became known for its saloons and brothels, but there was also a demand for more formal relationships. In 1862, one shipment of single women was sent over from England (in the care of and vouched for by a clergyman) to redress the balance of the population. Mail-order brides were not unknown, and weddings were quickly arranged upon their arrival.

The custom of throwing rice was taken a little too literally at one wedding. A well-heeled miner was married at the St. James Club when, at his very expensive and expansive wedding supper, he was caught in the face with a rice pudding.

ELEGANT RICE PUDDING

Everyday rice pudding was occasionally served for festive occasions, but it was dressed with a topping of meringue. We have no idea if this pudding was what was actually thrown at the wedding, but it's certainly worth serving at home.
Serves 4.

½ cup pudding (pearl) rice
⅓ cup brown sugar
1¼ cups light cream
1¼ cups milk
2 Tbsp butter, melted
2 egg yolks, beaten
½ tsp grated nutmeg
pinch salt
4 egg whites
4 Tbsp sugar

- Preheat oven to 325°.
- Grease a casserole dish, and place rice in the bottom of the dish.
- Combine cream, sugar, milk, melted butter, beaten egg yolks, nutmeg and salt, and pour over rice. Stir and bake for 2 hours.
- Whisk egg whites until thick and foamy, gradually add sugar and beat until stiff and peaks hold.
- Pile on top of the rice pudding.
- Increase the oven temperature to 350°. Bake for a further 20 to 30 minutes, until the top of the meringue is golden.

4

Heritage City

In 1853, the Victoria townsite was laid out by surveyors. Government, Bastion, Broughton and Wharf streets cuddled cosily around the fort, and the other roads ran from there. Little wooden shops sprang up — the British didn't use the word "store" — where merchants and shoppers lazily swapped stories while doing the daily rounds. The town expanded gradually into what is now known as "The Old Town," but still retained its relaxed character. By the turn of the century Emily Carr commented that "Victoria was like a laying down cow, chewing."

Stroll around the Old Town district and read the information plaques placed on many of the restored historic buildings. Watch for the old-fashioned road surface in Waddington Alley, where the traditional wooden cobbles really bring the past to life. Many of the elegant buildings that now house trendy boutiques and clothing stores were warehouses, fishmongers, ship chandlers and grocers. People it in your mind with the bustle and voices of women shopping for fish and meat, goods being unloaded at the dock, the smell of sawdust from the floor of the butcher's shop and the aroma of fresh bread baking.

Traffic now whizzes through Old Town and roars across the Johnson Street bridge, but leisurely shopping is still possible even if the stores have changed. Several of the old arcades have boutiques and restaurants tucked away inside; there are interesting alleys and courtyards to stroll through; and Market Square, a restored complex of historic warehouses, is a delightful area where you can browse for books, eat tempting and filling vegetarian delicacies and buy anything from beads to banjos. Make a point of dropping in on a tiny store around the corner from Market Square on Pandora Street. Called Global Village, it's run by volunteers and carries crafts from Third World countries. This is where we have picked up startlingly different batik tablecloths and some fascinating folk-art candlesticks and bowls to grace our table.

❦

Bread Recipes

Other than sourdough and Johnny cake we don't know what specific bread recipes were used in early Victoria, but here's a couple of interesting recipes that have been around for a long time.

THE STAFF OF LIFE

Victoria's first bakery was opened next to the fort in 1858. Before that, bread was either home-baked or shipped in from Port Townsend in the United States. The settlers were delighted; so, by all accounts, were the Songhees, as it was reported that they liked to use the biscuit tins for the personal effects of their dead. Samuel Nesbitt, the baker, decided to expand, and he opened another bakery by Esquimalt Harbour, and promptly became "Purveyor of Bread and Biscuits to Her Majesties' Navy." The sailors were no doubt glad to have a source of fresh bread instead of their ships' biscuits. This was a hard-baked bread which lasted for months, but eventually became infested with weevils. The old salts coped with this by tapping the biscuits on the table so the weevils fell out.

Nesbitt's Bakeries prospered so well that he was able to build a $10,000 house, which the populace nicknamed "Cracker Castle."

WHOLE-WHEAT COFFEE CAN BREAD

This recipe was developed out of necessity, but is currently politically correct as it encourages recycling of coffee cans.
Makes 2 loaves.

3 cups all-purpose flour
3 cups whole-wheat flour
1½ tsp salt
2 pkgs active dry yeast
2½ cups warm water
¼ cup brown sugar
¼ cup butter

- In a large warmed bowl stir together 1 cup of the all-purpose flour and 1 cup whole-wheat flour, the salt, yeast and brown sugar.
- Stir in the warm water and beat until smooth.
- Melt butter, cool to lukewarm and mix in with the remaining whole-wheat flour.
- Gradually add the remaining all-purpose flour to make a stiff dough.
- Turn out onto a floured board and knead 5 to 10 minutes or until no longer sticky but smooth.
- Place in a greased bowl. Lightly butter top of dough, cover with clean towel and let rise until doubled in size, approximately 1½ hours.
- Punch down, turn out on lightly floured board and knead gently to remove air bubbles.
- Divide into two. Shape into 2 round balls.
- Place inside two well-greased 2 lb-size coffee cans. Let rise until doubled in size (approximately 40 minutes).
- Bake at 375° for 40 minutes or until loaves sound hollow when tapped.

VICTORIANS AND FOOD: JANE NESBITT

Mrs Jane (née Saunders) Nesbitt arrived in Victoria on the bride ship, and married Samuel Nesbitt, who opened the first bakery in Victoria. After her husband's death, she took over the running of his Fort Street bakery and was so successful that the business expanded until seven men were employed. She was a fair employer and allowed her workers to form The Practical Bakers Association, the first labour organization in Victoria, and presumably an ancestor of the Workingmen's Protective Association, founded in Victoria in 1879.

ANADAMA BREAD

An old-time American favourite that travelled up the west coast.
Makes 2 loaves.

5 cups all-purpose flour
1 cup corn meal
2 pkgs active dried yeast
2 tsp salt
2 cups warm water
5 Tbsp soft butter
½ cup molasses

- In a warmed bowl stir together 2 cups flour, the corn meal, yeast and salt.
- Add the warm water, butter and molasses and beat hard for 3 minutes.
- Mix in enough of the remaining flour to make a stiff dough.
- Turn out onto floured board. Knead until no longer sticky.
- Place in a greased bowl. Butter top lightly. Cover with a clean cloth and leave to rise in a warm place until doubled in size (approximately 1½ hours).
- Punch dough down. Turn out onto floured board. Knead a few times and divide in half, shape into two balls.
- Place balls in 2 greased loaf pans. Cover and let rise until doubled (approximately 45 minutes).
- Bake at 375° for 45 to 50 minutes or until loaves sound hollow when tapped.

Tantalizing Memories

Major Roger Monteith shared a vivid memory. "Those old grocers' stores were so totally different. There was nothing in the way of refrigeration; everything was put out openly. There'd be hams and bacon, and generally, barrels of English mixed biscuits, currants, raisins, huge cheeses and a variety of other things, including . . . a coffee grinder where they ground your coffee as you wanted it . . . Those places had a most enticing odour."

OLD-FASHIONED GINGER BISCUITS

Crackled and crunchy on the outside and slightly soft in the centre, just like grandma used to make. They came in wooden cases with metal edges, like a miniature tea chest, tipped on the slant so you could pick out as many as you needed.
Makes 40 cookies.

¾ cup shortening
1 cup sugar
1 egg
¼ cup molasses
2 cups all-purpose flour
2 tsp baking soda
¼ tsp salt
2 tsp ginger
1 tsp cinnamon
1 tsp cloves
extra sugar

- Cream together the shortening and 1 cup of sugar.
- Beat in the egg and molasses.
- In another bowl sift together the flour, soda, salt and spices. Blend into the creamed mixture.
- Shape into small balls. Roll in the extra sugar.
- Place 2 inches apart on a greased cookie sheet. Bake at 350° for 8 to 10 minutes (do not over bake — cookies should be still be slightly soft).
- Cool on baking sheet for 10 minutes before removing to racks.

Royal Representatives

In the early 1860s, a fire-prone mansion known as Cary Castle was built as a private house. It was eventually bought as the official residence of British Columbia's lieutenant governors, who serve as the Royal representatives to the province.

Events there have often included large balls for visiting dignitaries, and sometimes it was a struggle to find enough staff. The Marchioness of Dufferin and Alva, wife to the Governor General who visited Cary Castle in 1876, gave a glimpse of life behind the scenes.

"Fred Ward, who is 'housekeeper' has ordered up the prisoners from the Penitentiary to pluck chickens for the ball; it is the custom here, and when we walked into the ballroom, we found six more prisoners, with chains to their legs and an armed man standing over them, polishing the floor."

Cary Castle eventually burnt to the ground in 1899. All that remains is its entrance, which has been incorporated into the current Government House.

COQ AU VIN

A poultry classic suitable for serving peasant style accompanied by French bread to catch the gravy for the ordinary folks, or classic style with Spanish rice (see page 106) for visiting dignitaries.

Makes 4 servings.

2 Tbsp butter
2 Tbsp olive oil
12 pieces chicken, legs, thighs or breasts
¼ cup brandy
12 small white onions
½ lb small button mushrooms
2 large garlic cloves, minced
2 Tbsp flour
1 cup dry red wine
1 cup chicken stock
1 bay leaf
½ tsp fine herb (also called herb Provence)
salt and pepper
parsley, chopped

- In a large Dutch oven, heat the butter and oil.
- Brown chicken pieces well on all sides.
- Pour in brandy and flame. Remove chicken with a slotted spoon and set aside.
- Add the small onions to the pan and brown them.
- Add the whole mushrooms and the garlic, and sauté lightly.
- Stir in the flour, then add the wine and stock in a steady stream.
- Stir in the fine herb and bay leaf, add salt and pepper to taste.
- Return chicken to pan, cover and cook for about 45 minutes or until chicken is tender.
- Transfer to a deep serving platter or dish. Sprinkle with parsley and serve immediately.

VICTORIANS AND FOOD: CHARLES & LEAH ROGERS

The Rogers founded a store which is a treat not to be missed by any self-respecting chocaholic. Charles W. Rogers originally owned a fruit business on Government Street, but in 1888, after his marriage to Leah Morrison of James Bay, he started experimenting with candy and chocolate recipes. The 5-cent chocolates were custard creams as big as tea biscuits, and became favourites of both the Royal Navy and tourists, resulting in a reputation that spread like wildfire. Now known as Victoria creams (and considerably more than 5 cents), these chocolates are still a hot favourite.

The Rogers became exceedingly wealthy, but as their wealth accumulated, so did their eccentricities. They never spent money if they could avoid it and refused to install electricity, the telephone or even inside plumbing in their house. They hated banks, and stories flew around town of thousands of dollars hoarded in their home, so they lived in fear of holdups. In an effort to avoid trouble, Mrs. Rogers, carrying the day's take in a black bag, walked home a block ahead of her husband so as not to be recognized.

There was a card in the shop window that read "My candies are made in the morning and sold in the afternoon." That was if you were lucky. Sometimes Mr. Rogers locked the door in the face of his customers, or refused to sell them more than one box of candies.

Rogers Chocolates still flourishes on Government Street, but today's staff will be delighted to sell you as many boxes as you like. The Victoria creams are still enormous and come with a little card explaining that you can cut them in quarters to share. We've never tried it! The size is just fine by us.

Because of the fame of Rogers, Victoria and chocolate go together in many people's minds. Here are some wonderfully decadent chocolate recipes that incorporate chocolate and a Victoria ambience.

White chocolate clamshell with Victoria truffles and chocolate dipped strawberries,
Chocolate quiche

In 1898, no one left for the Klondike without a hefty load of supplies

WHITE CHOCOLATE CLAMSHELL
WITH STRAWBERRIES

A spectacular end to a dinner party. It's fiddly, but quite easy to make. Giant clamshells can be purchased in the several gift stores around town. If you don't want to use a real shell, a plastic or ceramic one can be used. Serves 4 to 6.

1 giant clamshell, approximately 10 inches across
¾ lb white chocolate
4 ozs dark chocolate
1 lb strawberries, washed and dried, but not hulled

- Cover the inside of the clamshell with a sheet of aluminum foil, molding it to the shape so it is smooth. Tuck the edges firmly over the edge of the clamshell.
- Cover a baking sheet with a layer of foil and place shell on it, foil side up.
- Cover a second baking sheet with foil for the strawberries.
- Chop white chocolate and melt gently in a double boiler.
- Pour melted chocolate inside the shell and tip around to cover.
- Use a pastry brush to smooth chocolate further over the foil form. Aim for ¼ inch thick. If you have difficulty getting the right thickness, cover shell with several thin layers, cooling shell in the fridge between applications. Pour out excess chocolate.
- Let shell harden for at least 2 hours in fridge.
- Scrape remaining white chocolate into a small bowl and save for repairs.
- Melt dark chocolate in double boiler.
- Holding each strawberry by the hull, dip into the dark chocolate and place immediately on the foil sheet. Cool in fridge.
- Carefully unmold shell before dinner. Release the edge foil and use it to lift the chocolate shell, then gently peel the foil from the chocolate. Melt the spare chocolate and use to repair any broken bits damaged in the unmolding process.
- Place chocolate clam on a plate (or flat mirror), fill with chocolate-dipped strawberries and arrange one or two around it. Garnish with a rose and serve with strong coffee. After the strawberries are eaten, break pieces off the shell to nibble.
- If you cannot bear to let your guests eat the clamshell, whisk it away, wipe it out, store in plastic bubble wrap in an airtight box in your freezer and use again. (Do eat it before it gets freezer burn.)

VICTORIA TRUFFLES

Pleasantly rich, smooth, velvety and dark like the air in Beacon Hill Park on a warm summer night.
Makes 24.

1⅔ cups heavy cream
7 Tbsp unsalted butter
1 lb dark or semi-sweet chocolate, chopped
4 Tbsp Grand Marnier
Cocoa powder for dusting

- Pour cream into thick-bottomed saucepan, add butter and warm until butter melts.
- Turn up heat, stirring constantly, and bring cream just to the boil.
- Remove immediately from heat. Add chocolate and stir until completely melted.
- Continue stirring until mixture begins to cool and thicken.
- Stir in the Grand Marnier, then cover mixture and place in fridge. Leave in fridge for at least 2 hours, but stir 2 or 3 times during this thickening process.
- To make truffles, prepare a baking tray by pouring in a layer of cocoa powder.
- Scoop up portions of the chocolate with a spoon, drop onto the cocoa powder and roll lightly into balls (dust palms of hands with cocoa powder to prevent sticking).
- Refrigerate truffles immediately.
- Lovely served in the white chocolate clamshell *(see page 39).*

CHOCOLATE QUICHE

The perfect excuse for yet another visit to the chocolate shop.
Makes 16 small, rich slices.

Crust
¾ cup all-purpose flour, sifted
pinch salt
¾ cup almonds, finely ground
¼ lb plus 2 Tbsp unsalted butter, very cold
1 egg yolk
ice water, as needed

- Preheat oven to 350°.

- Combine flour, salt and almonds in a bowl, cut in the chilled butter and rub into flour, with fingertips only, until fine breadcrumb stage.
- Beat egg yolk with 1 tablespoon ice water. Sprinkle over flour and gently work into dough until it handles into a ball. (Sprinkle on extra ice water if needed.)
- Generously flour a clean tea towel and roll out dough on it. Line an 11 inch quiche dish with the dough and press dough in to make a smooth crust (press any broken or cracked bits together).
- Place a sheet of greased baking parchment over the dough and fill with dried peas. Bake blind for 10 minutes. Remove peas and parchment and bake for a further 3 minutes. Cool.

Filling
18 ozs dark or semi-sweet chocolate
1¾ cups whipping cream
7 egg yolks

- Chop chocolate and melt in a double boiler.
- In a bowl, beat the eggs and cream together until well mixed.
- Beat in the melted chocolate and pour into baked quiche case.
- Bake at 350° for approximately 45 minutes until the top feels firm.
- Cool before serving, but serve at room temperature from quiche dish.
- Serving suggestion: serve slices on a plate drizzled with fresh raspberry coulis *(see page 137).*

(see page 137).

Caffeine Plus

Another old established business that is still around is Murchie's Tea and Coffee Ltd. We've been fans since we first visited Victoria, and for twenty years a highlight of our visits to Victoria would be the acquisition of a large supply of coffee beans to take back to Edmonton. The long drive back through the Rockies was always delightfully odoriferous; with the air so full of caffeine, we didn't have to drink the stuff to stay awake! Murchie's has been around since the turn of the century. Currently Murchie's is a sophisticated store on Government Street that handles an incredible variety of coffee beans and teas, complete with an area where you can sit down and snack on extremely wicked cakes while sampling the latest brew. Coffee aficionados, it's time to load up with fresh beans and try these recipes.

COCOA MINT COFFEE

Serves 2.

1½ cups hot strong coffee
¼ cup coffee liqueur
¼ cup crème de menthe
whipped cream

- Preheat 2 brandy glasses by filling with hot water. Drain.
- Mix the two liqueurs and divide between the two glasses.
- Pour in the hot coffee.
- Top with whipped cream.

MEXICAN COFFEE

Serves 4.

1½ cups hot strong black coffee
½ tsp cinnamon

- Stir above ingredients together and pour into 4 demitasse cups.

½ cup whipping cream
1 tsp sugar
¼ tsp nutmeg
¼ tsp cinnamon

- Whip cream, sugar and spices and float on top of spiced coffee.

COFFEE AND RUM PUNCH

Serves 16.

8 cups vanilla ice cream
4 cups hot extra-strong coffee
4 cups light rum
nutmeg, freshly ground

- Place ice cream in large punch bowl and stir in the hot coffee. Stir until the ice cream is dissolved.
- Stir in rum and sprinkle with nutmeg.

Boozing it Up

The drinking of alcohol has had its official ups and downs in Victoria, but despite prohibition and the temperance movements, saloons, pubs, breweries and moonshine-makers have flourished in one form or another. After the influx of the miners, Johnson Street became lined with "saloons and bawdy houses" and became an area that "nice women" avoided. However, that didn't stop the "nice women" from exchanging recipes for elderberry wine, tipsy cakes and that famous English dish, sherry trifle.

ANDREA'S SHERRY TRIFLE

Traditional trifle should not be too sweet and should not have jello or canned fruit anywhere near it! It was invented as a quick and easy way to use up stale cake and was definitely an "adults only" dessert. The addition of jello and canned fruit to the sponge base instead of sherry seems to have crept in in an effort to make it a family dish.

1 – 8 by 11 inch stale cake, pound cake or plain sponge cake
½ cup blackberry or strawberry jelly, sherry to taste, medium sweet
3 cups custard, made with Bird's custard powder
2 cups whipping cream
1 or 2 candied cherries
a little angelica

- Crumble the stale cake, add the blackberry jelly a teaspoon at a time and mix in with a fork alternately with a slurp of sherry (in the trifle, not you!). Trifle is not an exact science, as the amount of jam and sherry depends upon the dryness of the cake and personal taste.
- Continue working in the jam and sherry until the cake is moist and coloured, almost a lumpy paste but not sodden with liquid. You should definitely be able to taste the sherry over the jam.
- Spread the cake mixture in the bottom of your prettiest glass trifle bowl.
- Make up 3 cups of custard by following maker's instructions. Pour over the cake layer and leave to cool and set.
- Whip cream and spread over the cold custard layer.
- Cut cherries into quarters and the angelica into slivers. Dot the cherries randomly on top of the trifle and add two slivers of angelica on each side of each cherry piece, so they look like tiny flowers. This is just to add a little colourful decoration, not taste.
- Serve with fanfare of trumpets!

GOOD FOR WHAT ALES YOU

The first brewery in Victoria, the Lion, was producing ale by 1862 and advertised delivery of its "Treble X Family Ale" anywhere in the city for $2.00 per dozen. Inner town sales were through grocery stores, though later the brewery operated its own taproom, which became the Lion Saloon. At one time, a schooner of beer cost 5 cents.

Other breweries included the Empire and the Silver Spring. Breweries changed hands and names, burnt down and relocated, but there seems to always have been one since that time. Today the Lucky Lager plant is producing beer from the same site as the historic Victoria Phoenix Brewery.

BEER, APRICOT AND NUT LOAF

The yeast in beer makes a raising ingredient with a tang for a very quick "quick bread" recipe.
Makes 1 loaf.

2¼ cups all-purpose flour
4 tsp baking powder
1 tsp salt
1 cup sugar
⅓ cup shortening
2 eggs
1 cup beer
½ cup pecans, chopped
1 cup dried apricots, chopped

- Grease and flour a 9 by 5 inch loaf pan.
- Sift together the flour, salt, baking powder and sugar.
- Lightly rub or cut in the shortening.
- In a small bowl, beat the eggs with the beer.
- Add the liquid to the dry ingredients, stirring only till combined. Batter will be lumpy.
- Stir in nuts and apricots.
- Pour into prepared pan and bake at 350° for 55 to 60 minutes or until a cake tester comes out clean. (If bread is colouring too much on top, loosely cover with foil.)

OLD-FASHIONED MULLED CIDER

Winter here is often wet and a cold damp lingers in the bones. Heart-warming drinks have been a Victoria tradition for many years. Apple cider, both alcoholic and nonalcoholic, has been produced here since the first fruit trees were grown by Fort Victoria personnel.
Serves 10.

8 cups apple cider or apple juice
2 lemons, thinly sliced
4 whole cloves
1 nutmeg, crushed
4 whole allspice
4 cinnamon sticks
1 cup brandy

- Tie spices in a muslin or cheesecloth bag.
- Combine all ingredients except the brandy in a large pot.
- Simmer gently for 20 minutes to meld flavours.
- Stir in brandy and ladle into punch glasses.

5

~~~

City in the Country

Despite becoming a bustling town, Victoria kept a lot of "country elegance." Even at the turn of the century, almost every home had some land attached, and that usually meant a horse, a cow and often chickens were kept "in the top section," even within the downtown area. Labour came cheap, and many established settlers could afford farm help and $25 a month for a live-in Chinese servant to help around the house. This made time for recreation, carriage rides to local beauty spots, picnics, riding parties and social teas, as reported by Lieutenant Richard Mayne of the Royal Navy.

"In fine weather, riding parties of the gentlemen and ladies of the place were formed, and we returned generally to a high tea or dinner tea at Mr. Douglas or Mr. Works [the Hudson's Bay Company chief trader] winding up a pleasant evening with dance and song."

High tea was a much more solid meal than afternoon tea. No delicate sandwiches, but hearty dishes such as cold meat pies and great platters of sliced meats, a variety of homemade pickles, breads, cakes and puddings as well as vegetables and salads and whole cheeses. As for the picnics, they had to be seen to be believed. Often ten to twenty people, and sometimes as many as forty, went either on horseback or in carriages. The servants would be sent ahead with not only the food, but also tables, chairs, linen cloths and napkins; teapots and spirit lamps on which to boil the water; china tea services; and, of course, drink. We have found passing reference to the following dishes in reports of various outings around Victoria.

Not having servants, you might not wish to cart everything out into the country, but these recipes make a delightful menu for summer's evening entertaining on the deck. Purchase some extra-large glass oil lamp funnels from that old Victoria establishment Capital Iron, and place them over your candlesticks for added Victorian elegance and practicality as a wind shield.

ROAST GLAZED HAM

Served hot or cold at High Tea, or taken on an elaborate picnic, ham has remained a choice way of feeding large gatherings.

1 precooked ham
whole cloves

- Score ham in diamond pattern. Insert cloves at corners of the diamonds.
- Bake in oven at 325° for 1 hour.
- Remove from oven, increase oven temperature to 450° and prepare the glaze.

Glaze
3 cups brown sugar, lightly packed
3 tsp mustard
2 Tbsp corn syrup
3 Tbsp flour
¼ cup red wine vinegar

- Mix together and spread over the top surface of the ham.
- Return to the oven and bake for 30 minutes or until glaze threads from a spoon.
- Remove from oven, but keep basting until glaze cools and hardens over ham.
- As a special touch, a decoration of sliced pineapple rings and glazed cherries could be put on the ham and the glaze poured over it. But you have to work extremely quickly.

HAVE SOME MADEIRA, MY DEAR

Flanders and Swann's song is a highly appropriate comment for a Victorian picnic, as the drink menu considered suitable for an outing was rather incredible by today's standards. Booze was taken not by the bottle, but by the basketful. One Victorian list suggested:

"Beverages — three dozen quarts of ale packed in hampers, ginger beer, soda water, and lemonade, of each two dozen bottles. Six bottles of claret, champagne at discretion, and any other white wine that may be preferred, two bottles of Madeira and two bottles of brandy."

A Piece of the Pie

Pies were a favourite choice for either savoury or dessert dishes. Here's a never-fail recipe that can be used for either.

NEVER-FAIL SHORT CRUST PASTRY

½ lb lard
2½ cups flour
½ tsp salt
½ tsp baking powder
½ cup of liquid comprising:
    1 small egg, beaten
    1 tsp brown sugar
    1 tsp vinegar
    ice water

- Mix the beaten egg, sugar and vinegar with a fork. Add enough water to make ½ a cup.
- Sift dry ingredients together.
- Cut in lard until like breadcrumbs. Mix in liquid quickly and lightly with a fork.
- Gather together into a ball. Chill till ready to use.

OLD ENGLISH FISH PIE

Yet another way of preparing the fish that was present in one form or another almost every day in Victoria households. Can be served hot or cold. This was also a popular dish on "meatless Fridays" or in Lent.
Serves 6 to 8.

Pastry
Never-fail Pastry Recipe *(see page 48)*

Filling
1 lb cod fillets
2 large onions
4 eggs, hard-boiled
1 cup mushrooms, sliced
2 Tbsp parsley, chopped
3 cloves
2 tsp mustard powder
2 tsp anchovy fillets, chopped
2 to 3 tsp hot water
1 egg, beaten
salt and pepper, to taste
2 tsp butter

- Cut ball of short crust pastry in half. Roll each half to fit the base and crust of an 8 inch pie dish.
- Fit base in the pie dish and chill.
- Preheat oven to 350°.
- Steam cod, remove bones and skin, flake.
- Peel and slice the onions.
- Shell and slice the hard-boiled eggs.
- Place in the pastry case layers of fish, onions, mushrooms and egg, sprinkling salt, pepper, mustard, cloves, parsley and chopped anchovies between the layers.
- Pour over hot water, dot with knobs of butter and place crust on top, sealing well and making a rim around the dish. Vent with a hole in the middle.
- Brush with beaten egg.
- Bake for 1 hour in lower part of oven. If pastry browns too quickly, cover loosely with foil.
- Serve hot or cold with pickles.

PICKLED ONIONS

Still a favourite with some British settlers.
Makes approximately 6 cups.

2½ lbs small yellow onions
8 cups boiling water
¾ cup coarse pickling salt
3 cups malt vinegar
1 cup water
1 cup granulated sugar
1 Tbsp mixed pickling spice

• Boil a kettle full of water, pour over onions and let stand for
  4 minutes.
• Drain, cover with cold water. Let stand for 4 minutes. Drain and
  peel.
• Combine 8 cups of boiling water with pickling salt. Pour this brine
  over the onions. Let stand overnight.
• Drain, rinse with cold water several times. Drain again.
• Combine vinegar, 1 cup of water, and sugar in a large saucepan.
• Drop in the pickling spices, tied in cheesecloth.
• Bring to the boil and boil, covered, for 5 minutes.
• Remove cheesecloth bag.
• Add onions and simmer, covered, for 5 minutes.
• Pack into hot sterilized canning jars. Cover with hot liquid and
  seal according to lid instructions.
• Store in cool dark place.

PICKLED BEETS

*Beets grow particularly well in the fertile Victoria soil. Don't throw away
the tender tops, as they are also a very tasty vegetable. Steam the greens and
toss with butter or a little olive oil, salt and pepper.*
Makes approximately 4 cups.

2 lbs small beets
1½ cups cider vinegar
½ cup water
1 cup brown sugar

• Precook beets in salted water for 20 minutes. Peel beets. Quarter
  any of the bigger beets.

- Pack into hot sterilized jars.
- In a large saucepan combine vinegar, water and sugar, and simmer for 5 minutes.
- Pour hot vinegar over beets to cover completely, but leaving required head space.
- Seal jars according to lid instructions.
- Store in cool dark place.

BREAD AND BUTTER PICKLES

Perfect with fresh bread and cold meat slices.
Makes 10 cups.

3½ lbs small cucumbers
1½ cups onion, chopped
1 green pepper, diced
½ cup pickling salt
3 cups white vinegar
3 cups sugar
2 tsp mustard seeds
1 tsp celery seeds
1 tsp turmeric

- Wash cucumbers and slice ⅛ inch thick.
- In a large bowl combine cucumbers, onions, green pepper and salt.
- Cover and let stand at room temperature for 12 hours.
- Drain off liquid and rinse well with cold water. Drain again.
- In a large saucepan, combine vinegar, sugar and spices.
- Bring to the boil.
- Add drained cucumber mixture and return to full boil.
- Pack cucumber mixture into hot sterilized jars. Pour liquid over, covering completely but leaving required head space.
- Seal according to lid instructions.
- Store in cool dry place.

BUBBLE BREAD

The traditional name is monkey bread, but no one knows why. Now known as Bubble Bread, it's easy for picnics as the "bubbles" pull apart and the amount of butter in the recipe means they don't need buttering.
Makes about 35 small pull-apart buns.

1 pkg active dry yeast
1 tsp sugar
½ cup lukewarm water
1 cup milk
1 cup butter
¼ cup granulated sugar
1½ tsp salt
3 eggs, beaten
5½ cups all-purpose flour (approximately)

- Place the 1 teaspoon of sugar into a large bowl, add the water and stir until dissolved.
- Sprinkle the yeast on top and let stand until frothy (approximately 10 minutes).
- Heat milk with ½ cup of butter until butter dissolves. Remove from heat and keep stirring until lukewarm. Stir into the yeast mixture.
- Beat the ¼ cup sugar, salt and eggs together and then beat into the yeast mixture. Beat well.
- Gradually beat in enough flour to make a soft dough. Turn onto floured surface and knead until smooth and elastic (approximately 10 minutes).
- Place in a greased bowl, turning to grease all surfaces. Cover and let rise until doubled in bulk (1 to 1½ hours).
- Punch down and roll out to half thick. Cut into 2 inch squares.
- Melt remaining butter, cool to lukewarm.
- Dip squares completely in butter, shake off excess and arrange in layers in a buttered 10 inch tube pan. Cover and let rise until doubled in bulk (approximately 1 hour).
- Bake at 375° for 45 minutes or until bread sounds hollow when tapped. If top starts to overbrown, cover loosely with foil.

MIXED BEAN SALAD

This is a modern recipe; obviously the canned vegetables can be replaced with fresh, cooked just to tender crisp, if you wish to be authentic.
Makes 12 servings.

1 can (14 ozs) cut green beans
1 can yellow wax beans
1 can red kidney beans
1 can chick peas
1 cup celery, chopped
1 red onion, thinly sliced, made into rings
½ cup green pepper, chopped
⅔ cup sugar
⅔ cup tarragon vinegar
⅔ cup olive oil
1 tsp salt
1 tsp ground pepper
1 tsp fresh dill
1 tsp basil, chopped
1 garlic clove, chopped (optional)

- Drain the cans of beans. Rinse with cold water and drain again.
- Combine all beans and chopped vegetables in a large bowl.
- In a smaller bowl, whisk together the sugar, vinegar, oil, herbs, garlic and seasonings.
- Pour dressing over vegetables and toss well. Check seasoning and adjust to taste.
- Cover salad and marinate in fridge for at least 8 hours or overnight. It will keep for several days. Toss occasionally.
- Drain before serving.

STRAWBERRY AND RHUBARB
MERINGUE TOPPED TARTS

Dressed up with meringue bonnets, an old favourite has a new look. We are not sure how they transported these, but if you have several carriages for the equipment anything is possible.
Makes 12 to 14 tarts.

3 cups strawberries, sliced
1 cup rhubarb, sliced
3 tsp water
1 tsp lemon juice
1 cup sugar
1 tsp cornstarch
12 to 14 – 3 inch baked tart shells
2 egg whites
½ cup sugar
pinch salt

- Place sliced strawberries and rhubarb in a saucepan with the lemon juice and 2 teaspoons of the water. Simmer for 10 minutes, but do not boil.
- Add sugar and simmer for another 10 minutes, stirring occasionally.
- In a small bowl dissolve the cornstarch with the remaining teaspoon of water. Stir into the fruit and simmer while stirring until the mixture thickens (approximately 2 to 3 minutes).
- Remove from heat and let cool. Spoon into the prebaked pastry shells.
- Whip egg whites until frothy, add salt and sugar and beat until they hold stiff peaks.
- Spoon meringue on top of fruit tarts, making sure you seal to the pastry edges.
- Bake at 350° until meringue turns golden.

Snow peas and cauliflower salad with lemon dressing, Steak and kidney pie with Never-fail short crust pastry, Roast leg of lamb, Fatless roast potatoes

At the turn of the century, meat delivery was not very hygienic

MADEIRA CAKE

This classic plain cake, without any adornment, was cut in small slices and served with glasses of Madeira wine, hence its name. It travels well for picnics.

1 cup butter
1 cup sugar
2 cups flour
2 tsp baking powder
2 eggs
1 tsp grated zest of lemon
¼ to ½ cup milk (approximately)
1 Tbsp sugar
slivers of candied lemon peel

- Grease and flour a 7 inch loaf tin.
- Cream together butter and sugar until soft and light.
- Sift together flour and baking powder.
- Beat eggs in small bowl.
- Add eggs and flour alternately to butter mixture.
- Stir in lemon zest and enough milk to give the mixture a soft consistency.
- Sprinkle the tablespoon of sugar on surface and place slivers of candied lemon in a design.
- Bake at 375° for 1½ hours

MONSTER OR MYTH?

A favourite place for outings was Cadboro Bay, where people flocked hoping to sight the "Cadborosaurus" sea monster. The sightings started in 1928 and by 1959 over six hundred people had reported seeing some kind of incredible creature. We note without comment that the main rash of sightings also coincided with the fashion for elaborate picnics with lots of alcoholic refreshments.

SUMMER PUDDING

Blackberrying was, and still is, a favourite pastime and a good excuse for a summer outing. What better way to enjoy the taste of fresh berries than in old-fashioned Summer Pudding? Use day-old (or even older) firm, dense white bread, or the pudding will be mushy.
Serves 8.

1 lb fresh blackberries, washed and well drained
2 large tart apples (Granny Smith)
1½ cups sugar
1 orange, grated rind and juice
1 loaf day-old bread, thickly sliced (at least 12 slices)
1 cup whipping cream

- Grate rind on the orange, squeeze for the juice and set both aside.
- Peel, core and slice apples.
- Place apple slices in a saucepan with 1 cup of the blackberries, the orange rind and sugar.
- Add enough water to the orange juice to bring it to 2 cups, and add to the saucepan.
- Bring quickly to the boil, reduce heat and simmer (stirring often) until the apples are soft and the liquid is syrupy.
- Drain syrup and reserve.
- Stir cooked fruit into fresh fruit and let stand until cooled.
- Cut crusts off bread slices, and cut each slice in half (make rectangles).
- Completely line the bottom and sides of an 9 inch round casserole dish with the bread, trimming the slices to fit where necessary. Reserve all the offcuts.
- Moisten the bread lining by spooning on some of the reserved syrup.
- Spread a quarter of the fruit over the bottom of the lining.
- Cover with more bread slices and moisten with syrup, repeating until all the fruit is used.
- Top with a layer of bread and pour on the remaining syrup. Let it stand for 30 minutes to absorb.
- Place a small plate (one that fits inside the rim of the dish) on top of the pudding and cover the whole with plastic wrap. Place a medium weight on top of the plate (a can of fruit works) and chill overnight.
- Just before serving, remove wrap and plate, invert on top of a large platter with a rim to catch any juice. Serve with whipped cream.

CANOES, CREAM AND STRAWBERRIES

The Gorge was "the place" for a weekend outing by water. Victorians rented canoes from McIntosh's Boathouse on the Inner Harbour, and paddled up the arm of the Gorge to visit friends in the beautiful houses on the banks. This became such a popular pastime that the Queen's birthday (May 24) became marked by "The Gorge Regatta," with canoe races and greasy pole climbing competitions. The big houses on the shore threw open their grounds and served freshly picked strawberries, cream and tea. A place on the Gorge called Victoria Gardens became a favourite courting spot; couples could paddle up in the early evening and while away a couple of hours dancing in the moonlight, augmented by Chinese paper lanterns hanging from the trees. Though the tea gardens are long gone, the Gorge is still a beautiful place to canoe, and the picturesque walks along the bank are well worth exploring.

CANOE SUNDAE

Perfect for a little togetherness.

1 banana
3 scoops different ice creams
to taste strawberries, sliced
to taste Triple Sec
to taste whipped cream
to taste chocolate, grated
   or nuts, chopped

- In a boat-shaped glass bowl, carefully slice 1 banana lengthwise and lay the halves along the sides of the bowl.
- Fill centre with 3 scoops of different flavoured ice creams.
- Top with sliced strawberries.
- Drizzle with a fruit-flavoured liqueur, such as Triple Sec.
- Top with whipped cream.
- Sprinkle with grated chocolate or chopped nuts.
- Serve with 2 spoons, preferably on a deck under the stars.

SULTANA FRUITCAKE

A version of this was famous throughout Victoria. It was made by the Fernwood Bakery and served at the Japanese Tea Gardens on the Gorge. As late as 1989, it was reported that the turn-of-the-century brick Dutch oven used for baking the cake was still in the original building on Fernwood Road. This recipe makes a very elegant, light fruitcake that can be served at Christmas for those who don't like heavy fruitcake.
Makes 2 fruitcakes that keep well.

2 lbs sultanas (light raisins)
1 lb candied cherries
1 cup almonds, ground
3 cups all-purpose flour
1 cup butter
1⅓ cups sugar
2 tsp almond flavouring
4 eggs, separated
⅓ cup brandy
⅓ cup milk
½ tsp cream of tartar

- Grease two 7 inch cake pans and line with 2 layers of baking parchment.
- Combine sultanas, cherries and ground almonds with ½ cup of the flour, and toss together.
- Cream the butter and sugar and almond flavouring.
- Separate the eggs.
- Gradually beat the egg yolks into the creamed mixture until light and fluffy.
- Mix together the brandy and milk.
- Add the remaining flour alternately with the brandied milk to the creamed mixture.
- Beat egg whites with cream of tartar until stiff peaks form.
- Fold into the batter.
- Stir in the floured fruit.
- Bake at 300° for approximately 2½ hours or until the cakes test done with a toothpick.
- Remove from pan, peel off paper, cool.

~~~

Fresh Produce

Victoria is still "the city in the country," as it is largely surrounded by bountiful farmland. This means fresh fruits and vegetables are always at hand. A popular afternoon out today may involve driving to one of the many farms that offer "pick it yourself" deals. There is nothing like spending a sweaty day in the fields, filling baskets and boxes of fresh fruits and vegetables for the home freezer, to make you feel as though you live in a rural area. At the start of the growing season a four-page flyer is sent around Victoria, listing the farms, their addresses and the best time to go and pick produce ranging from early strawberries and raspberries through to the fall pumpkins. It also lists the farmers' markets where fresh produce is available for those who like life just a little easier.

For those who prefer pursuing wild plant life, the blackberries are a delicious August treat. Hanging over fences, abounding at the bottom of gardens and running wild in roadside ditches, they can be seen everywhere. We suggest a drive out to some of the more natural areas where there is less danger of the blackberries having been sprayed.

Here are some unusual but simple vegetable recipes that take full advantage of abundant offerings from farms on the Saanich Peninsula and the Metchosin and Sooke areas.

ASPARAGUS WITH MUSTARD CREAM SAUCE

A sure sign of spring, the tender shoots of asparagus are enhanced by sauce with a subtle bite.

Serves 4 as a vegetable.

1 lb asparagus, washed and trimmed
2 Tbsp butter
¼ cup whipping cream
1 tsp Dijon mustard
salt and pepper, to taste
chives, chopped

- Steam asparagus until tender. Place in warm serving dish and keep hot.
- In a saucepan, melt the butter, stir in mustard.
- Stirring all the time, pour in the cream and add the salt and pepper.
- Bring gently to the boil, stirring until very thick.
  Pour over asparagus, sprinkle with chopped chives.

CARROT TIMBALES

An interesting and colourful addition to a dinner, these are easy to make and can be made ahead and reheated in the moulds in a water bath.
Serves 8 as a vegetable helping.

1½ lbs carrots, peeled and sliced
3 Tbsp butter, at room temperature
4 eggs
1 tsp salt
pepper, to taste
¼ tsp ground nutmeg
½ tsp ground ginger
¾ cup whipping cream
3 Tbsp chopped dill or fennel

- Prepare moulds. Butter 8 Pyrex custard cups. Cut circles of waxed paper to fit in the bottom of the cups. Butter circles.
- Steam sliced carrots until tender. Reserve 8 slices and purée rest in a food processor.
- While processor is running, blend in the butter. Add eggs one at a time. Add cream and the seasonings and spices except for the dill.
- Taste mixture and adjust seasoning.
- Spoon mixture into moulds. Place moulds in a large baking dish. Fill baking dish with boiling water until it reaches halfway up the sides of the cups.
- Bake at 350° for 35 to 40 minutes or until carrot is firm to the touch.
- Remove moulds from water bath, run a knife around their edges and leave to rest for 5 minutes. Turn out onto a serving dish. Lift off paper.
- Garnish each timbale with a slice of the reserved carrot and some chopped dill.

HERBED RED POTATO SALAD

Tossing the hot potatoes in the dressing allows them to absorb the flavours.
Serves 8 to 10.

8 new red potatoes, unpeeled
1 large sprig of fresh mint
salt, to taste

- Boil potatoes with mint in a large saucepan of salted water until tender.
- Drain.

Dressing
⅓ cup tarragon vinegar
1 Tbsp Dijon mustard
½ cup corn oil
⅓ cup olive oil
1 tsp salt
¼ tsp pepper
¼ cup fresh herbs — e.g. mint, thyme, savory, basil, oregano — chopped

• Whisk vinegar and mustard together in a large bowl.
• Gradually whisk in the two oils until thickened.
• Stir in salt, pepper and herbs.
• Cut the hot potatoes into ¼ inch slices, leaving the skins on for colour.
• Add to the dressing and toss gently.
• Cover and refrigerate until cold. (Leave no longer than 4 hours.)
• Toss again before serving.

SNOW PEAS AND CAULIFLOWER SALAD

The lemony dressing really complements the simple cauliflower.
Serves 10.

2 heads cauliflower
2 cups snow peas
¼ cup green onions, chopped
1 red pepper, chopped
1 yellow pepper, chopped
¼ cup sesame seeds

Dressing
½ cup corn oil
⅓ cup sour cream
¼ cup lemon juice
1 garlic clove, minced

• Cut cauliflower into florets and steam until tender crisp. Cool under cold running water, drain and dry.
• Top and tail snow peas and blanch in boiling water for 2 minutes. Rinse under cold water, drain and dry.
• Mix all vegetables in a large salad bowl.
• In a small bowl whisk sour cream and lemon juice, then add the oil gradually in a stream. Stir in the garlic.

- Pour dressing over vegetables. Toss, cover and refrigerate for 2 hours.
- Toss again before serving and sprinkle with sesame seeds.

PUMPKIN SOUP

Delicious and filling, this soup makes a meal on its own served with warm fresh bread. It's also a spectacular start to a formal dinner when served ladled from the pumpkin shell. There are several pumpkin farms by the Pat Bay Highway that are worth driving past in October . . . acre after acre of bright orange globes. Beautiful!
Serves 6 to 8 as part of a dinner, 3 to 4 as a complete meal.

1 large pumpkin, approximately 5 lbs
4 cups water
1/4 cup butter
1 large onion, sliced
1 cup whipping cream
salt, to taste
1/2 tsp pepper
1 tsp nutmeg
1 tsp coriander
1 green onion, chopped

- Wash and dry the pumpkin. Cut through to the inside, in a circle about 8 inches in diameter, around the stem. Lift off top.
- Remove and discard all seeds and stringy pith.
- Using a very sharp knife, carefully remove the pumpkin pulp, leaving a 1/2 inch-thick layer. Work slowly and carefully so you don't puncture the skin.
- Chop the pulp.
- Melt the butter in a large saucepan, add the onion and sauté until transparent.
- Add the chopped pulp and the water. Bring to the boil and then turn down heat, cover and simmer gently for 30 minutes.
- Purée mixture in food processor in several small batches, and return to saucepan.
- Stir in the cream, salt, pepper, nutmeg and coriander. Taste, and adjust salt accordingly.
- Reheat and pour into the pumpkin shell.
- Sprinkle chopped green onion on top.

RASPBERRY MOUSSE

Like the fruit, our raspberry season is short and sweet. As we never get enough of them, it's almost sacrilege to eat raspberries any other way than fresh with a little cream. However, this recipe keeps the sweet sharp flavour intact.
Serves 8.

4 cups fresh raspberries
¾ cup sugar
2 Tbsp raspberry liqueur or cherry brandy
1 Tbsp lemon juice
2 pkgs unflavoured gelatin
1 cup whipping cream
2 egg whites

- Prepare a 6 inch soufflé dish by taping a 3 inch doubled foil collar around the upper rim.
- In a food processor, blend the raspberries till smooth, press through a sieve to remove seeds. Pour 2 cups of purée in a saucepan.
- Add ½ cup of the sugar. Stir over low heat for barely 5 minutes or until the sugar has dissolved.
- Stir in the liqueur and lemon juice and transfer to a bowl.
- Pour ½ cup of water in a saucepan, sprinkle in the gelatin and let stand to soften. After 1 minute heat gently until gelatin has dissolved. Stir into raspberry mixture.
- Place bowl into larger bowl containing water and ice cubes. Chill for approximately 20 minutes, stirring frequently. By this time contents should have the consistency of raw egg white.
- While raspberry is cooling, whip cream and set aside.
- Whip egg whites with remaining sugar until stiff peaks form.
- Whisk ⅓ of the egg white into the raspberry mixture, then gently fold the raspberry mixture and the whipped cream into the remaining whites.
- Pour into prepared soufflé dish (mixture should be up above rim and supported by collar).
- Chill in fridge for at least 6 hours.
- To serve, gently undo collar and peel back. Pipe extra whipping cream rosettes around rim and rough edge and serve immediately.

BLACKBERRY SURPRISES

When there is a glut of blackberries, your freezer is full, you've made pies, jam and jelly and you need some ideas to get rid of the ones that keep persistently ripening at the bottom of the garden, here are some suggestions.

- Add blackberries to glasses of lemonade.
- Make blackberry vinegar for salad dressings.
- Boil blackberries with water and sugar and make instant pancake syrup.
- Sprinkle a handful of blackberries on spinach salad.
- Blackberries and ice cream on waffles.
- The raspberry mousse recipe on page 63 also works with blackberries.

Our favourite? Use blackberries instead of blueberries in muffins.

6

Tourist City

By the turn of the century the swelling population of Victoria had caused an unpleasant side effect. The James Bay mud flats became a dumping ground for all kinds of rubbish, and the smell was appalling. Citizens used the rickety bridge across the flats as a drop-off point for everything from kitchen and personal waste to dead horses. The population rejoiced when, in 1904, a motion was passed, the mud flats were gradually filled in, the bridge replaced by a concrete causeway, and what is now a grand old Victoria Tourist Institution started to rise from the sludge – the Empress Hotel.

It's hard to equate the elegant harbourfront and James Bay area with the accounts of the mud that preceded the upgrading. The Empress wasn't the only new construction site. Saloons, multi-balconied hotels, new sidewalks, warehouses and homes caused chaos with unexpected holes in the ground. Victoria became a nightmare after dark as citizens fell into potholes and excavations at regular intervals. To remind us of Victoria's tourist beginnings, we couldn't resist Mud Pie.

MUD PIE À LA JAMES BAY

Serves 8 to 10.

Crust
22 Oreo cookies
2 Tbsp butter, melted

- Use a food processor to blend cookies until like fine breadcrumbs.
- Mix with melted butter.

- Press crumbs into a 10 inch pie plate and freeze.

Mud

1 qt chocolate ice cream, softened
1 qt coffee ice cream, softened
2 Tbsp instant coffee granules
3 Tbsp Tia Maria
3 Tbsp brandy
1 cup whipping cream
dark chocolate, grated

- Place softened ice creams in a large bowl.
- In a small bowl mix together the Tia Maria, brandy and coffee granules until coffee dissolves.
- Pour liquid over the ice cream and swirl everything together. Make sure the liquid is mixed in, but a streaky effect with the ice cream is pretty.
- Pour the mixture into the frozen cookie crust and freeze solidly.
- After the first hour lay a covering of freezer or plastic wrap over the top so the ice cream doesn't absorb any flavours from the freezer.
- Remove from freezer approximately 15 minutes before serving.
- Decorate with whipped cream and shavings of dark chocolate.

The Empress Reigns

Right from its start, the Empress Hotel was destined for greatness. Designed as "a fitting companion to the historic pile on the heights of Quebec," she was part of a plan by architect Francis M. Rattenbury that revamped the James Bay mud flats by building a new post office at one end of the causeway, the legislature at the other, with the Empress in the middle, dominating the Inner Harbour like a dowager at the head of a dinner table. She was irresistible. The first guest checked in on January 20, 1908, and by the time dinner was served at 7 PM her reputation was secured.

Tourists came on early cruise ships, small ones that anchored at the Inner Harbour immediately in front of her; royalty passed through her imposing entrance; the élite of Victoria graced her balls and tea dances; and, to this day, you have to fight for a reservation for afternoon tea in the lobby.

The dinner dances were legendary. For $2 a couple you could dine on consommé, chicken à la king, ice cream parfait and coffee, then dance all night to Billy Tickle and his Toe Tappers.

The Empress also gradually attracted a resident population of elderly ladies who rented rooms on a permanent basis. Known as "The Empress dowagers," some fell on hard times during the Depression and went to great lengths to preserve their lifestyle by economizing on food. To do this they smuggled hot plates into their rooms. In true Empress fashion a blind eye was drawn, though one dowager was asked not to make strawberry jam on her hot plate, another gently restrained from cooking liver and onions, and a third from pickling onions.

BAKED LIVER AND ONIONS

Here is a liver recipe that is not quite as odoriferous as the smell of fried liver and onions that once floated down the Empress's corridor. In fact the liver is both tasty and tender.
Serves 3 to 4.

1 lb liver, sliced
⅓ cup flour
salt and pepper
½ tsp dried mustard
1 large onion, sliced
8 to 10 slices of bacon
1½ cups tomato juice
1 Tbsp ketchup

- Mix flour with the mustard and a good shaking of salt and pepper, dredge all sides of the liver.
- Arrange liver in a greased baking dish, cover with the sliced onions and bacon.
- Mix together the tomato juice and ketchup and pour over the contents of the baking dish.
- Bake at 300° for 1 hour.

CHICKEN À LA KING

A popular dish at the Empress dinner dances in the twenties and thirties. Serve it over toast for a lighter meal, or with rice and stir-fried veggies for something a little more substantial. Also stunning if served in a baked vol-au-vent case.

Serves 4.

¼ cup butter
1 garlic clove, chopped
3 Tbsp flour
1 can chicken bouillon
   or 1½ cups homemade chicken stock
½ cup milk (approximately)
2 cups chicken breast, cooked and cubed
1 cup peas, cooked
½ cup sliced mushrooms, cooked
½ tsp salt
¼ tsp pepper
dash red pepper sauce (optional)

- Melt butter in a saucepan and gently sauté the chopped garlic.
- Add the flour and stir till a smooth thickened roux.
- Mix the milk and bouillon to make 2 cups, gradually add this liquid to the flour mixture, blending and stirring constantly until there are no lumps.
- Cook slowly until the mixture thickens and makes a smooth sauce.
- Mix in all the remaining ingredients. Check seasoning and adjust.
- Cook gently until heated through.

~~~

Royal Visitors

Victoria has had no shortage of royal visitors, commencing in 1901 with the Duke & Duchess of Cornwall and York (later George V & Queen Mary), followed by several reigning monarchs. King George VI and Queen Elizabeth came in 1939, the present Queen and Prince Philip first in 1959. These visits were interspersed with various royal princes and princesses, Queen Elizabeth the Queen Mother, and also royalty from Denmark, Japan and the Netherlands.

Royal heirs tend to have more fun than the actual head of state, and the Prince of Wales (briefly Edward VIII then the Duke of Windsor) entertained Victorians in 1919, when a grand ball for more than a thousand people was given for him at the Empress. This was the only occasion on which the hotel has been open by invitation only. No less than three bands entertained the throng, and supper was served from a horseshoe-shaped buffet to three hundred dancers at a time. Salads, sandwiches, cakes, jellies, ice cream and coffee were served among rose-coloured chrysanthemums. The prince attempted to dance with as many of the ladies as possible, but still had a way to go when "God Save the King" was played at midnight. "Now we've put father to bed, let's get on with the dance," he loudly announced. Although history does not record when the festivities ended, the party obviously got livelier, for one MLA awoke the next morning to find himself sharing a bath with a live octopus.

VICTORIANS AND FOOD: BILLY TICKLE

He led the orchestra at the Empress from 1928 to 1960. To many people, Billy was the Empress. During the day he played in the lounge with the Billy Tickle Trio, and watched "a great many people put on a few pounds as they consume the famous crumpets and honey." To encourage this he played only tunes with a steady tempo!

At night, with an augmented band, he led Billy Tickle and his Toe Tappers, and was also unofficial chaperon to the young of Victoria. Anxious parents would phone him to inquire when (and with whom) their daughter had left the dinner dances.

But he was best known for steadfastly refusing to play "foreign" national anthems. Only "God Save the King" was ever played by his orchestra, no matter who was in the audience, and only six bars of that. When challenged, he would pull a tatty newspaper clipping from his breast pocket. This defined royal protocol – only six bars of the British national anthem unless the sovereign was present. Billy Tickle played "God Save the King" through for the first time in 1939, in the presence of George VI and Queen Elizabeth.

ROYAL GEM COOKIES

A fancy adaptation of plain old sugar cookies.
Makes 20 cookie "sandwiches".

1 cup butter
½ cup brown sugar, lightly packed
½ cup granulated sugar
1 egg
½ tsp vanilla
2 cups all-purpose flour
1 tsp baking soda
1 tsp cream of tartar

- Cream butter and both sugars until light and fluffy.
- Beat in the egg and vanilla.
- In another bowl, sift together the dry ingredients, gradually add to creamed ingredients until just blended. Wrap dough in waxed paper and chill for a couple of hours.
- Roll out dough to ¼ inch thick. Cut out circle shapes with a round cookie cutter. With a metal spatula, transfer half of them to an ungreased baking sheet. Cut out thimble-sized holes from the centre of the remaining circles. Transfer rings to a baking sheet.
- Bake at 375° for 8 minutes or until slightly brown. Cool on wire racks.
- When cool dip the rings into white icing made by combining icing sugar with a little water. Let dry.
- Spread strawberry jam on the circles and top with the white rings. The jam will make a nice gem in the centre.

⌒

Bengal Room

If you want to "do" the Empress, but wish to be a little more original than afternoon tea, try lunch in the Bengal Room. This is a sheer delight, colonialism gone mad, curry British pukka sahib style! The curry is dispensed from silver chafing dishes on a long oak and brass buffet. Line up and solemnly choose your curry, condiments and pappadams, and watch it served onto your plate by uniformed staff. Carry your plate back to the bamboo table and eat with silver tableware under a ceiling adorned with punkah fans and tent-like hangings reminiscent of Ghengis Khan. Watch your manners or you will be glared at by the

Ground lamb curry, pappadams and condiments

About 1902, the Ellsworthy and Boggs families got together for a family picnic with the help of their Chinese servant

tiger skin suspended over the fireplace. It's all magnificently silly and quite delicious.

GROUND LAMB CURRY

Serves 4.

¼ cup butter
3 large onions, chopped
2 tsp ginger root, grated
1 large garlic clove, crushed
1 tsp salt
1 lb ground lamb
1 tsp Garam Masala*
1 tsp turmeric
1 tsp ground cumin
1 tsp ground coriander
¼ tsp cayenne pepper
3 medium tomatoes, chopped
2 Tbsp plain yogurt
¼ cup water
3 Tbsp fresh cilantro/coriander

* *Garam Masala is a spice mix available at Asian stores. We found it plus many other exotic condiments and a wonderful variety of pappadams at a tiny store called B & V Market on Quadra Street.*

- Heat butter in a large heavy saucepan. Sauté 1 cup of onions, stirring constantly, until they are a rich brown (but not burnt), approximately 10 to 15 minutes. Remove with a slotted spoon and reserve.
- Add remaining onions, ginger, garlic and salt, stirring constantly. Fry for approximately 6 minutes until onions are soft and golden.
- Add lamb and continue stirring until the meat shows no pink.
- Stir in Garam Masala, turmeric, cilantro, cayenne, tomatoes, yogurt and water. Bring to the boil over high heat while stirring constantly. Reduce heat to simmer, cover tightly and simmer for 10 to 15 minutes.
- Wash, dry and chop cilantro leaves.
- Stir curry and check seasoning.
- Ladle in a deep heated bowl, sprinkle with chopped cilantro and the reserved fried onions.
- Serve with rice *(see page 128)* and pappadams.

PAPPADAMS

Also called popads, or poppadoms, these look like giant potato chips, but they are made of chick pea flour and spices. They can be fried in a little oil – heat the oil and press them down with a spatula for a few seconds, then turn and press again in the areas not cooked. Drain on a paper towel. They are eaten cold by breaking bits off with the fingers. A more modern way of cooking them that eliminates oil is in the micro-wave. Place a paper towel on the glass shelf. Place 1 pappadam on the towel and microwave on high for 30 seconds.

Tea Time

Afternoon tea at the Empress has been a tourist must for many years, but that's not where the locals go. They tend to gather at the Blethering Place in Oak Bay or in one of the other local teahouses dotted around the Victoria area. A favourite spot of ours is Point Ellice House.

Point Ellice House is so far off the beaten track you may think you are lost. The access road winds past beat-up cars and industrial sites before turning into Pleasant Street and meeting an old Victorian hidden gem, all that's left of a lovely and secluded little enclave of elegant houses built on Point Ellice around 1860.

We suggest you abandon your car in a downtown parking lot and be a real Victorian. Head down to the Inner Harbour and catch the tiny harbour ferry that goes up to the Gorge and stops at the Point Ellice Dock. Visitors arrived by boat when the O'Reilly family was in residence.

Members of the O'Reilly family lived here from 1861 to 1975. But in its heyday, when the original family was bringing up four daughters, the house was a social gathering place and a hot spot for croquet parties, tennis parties and teas. Now Point Ellice House is a heritage site complete with tour guides and interpretation (meet the Chinese servant in the kitchen for a real touch of authenticity). The afternoon tea program was developed in 1993 and was a rip-roaring success so you have to book ahead, but it's worth it. This is definitely one of the most authentic afternoon tea experiences we've found.

So, tongue firmly in cheek, we offer you a selection of "Do it Yourself" Victoria afternoon tea recipes. Do it properly though . . . white linen tablecloth, lace doilies (no paper ones, please), starched linen napkins and, of course, the best English china and a silver tea service with a choice of sugar and milk or lemon slices! Who knows, if you comb some of Victoria's antique shops you might find one of the traditional three-tiered cake servers. Serve the savouries on the top layer, the tiny cake slices and squares on the middle layer and the scones on the bottom, flanked by cut glass bowls containing jam and cream – don't forget an elegant posy of flowers as a centrepiece. See chapter 11, "City of Gardens," for some suggestions for enhancing your tea with edible flowers and floral butters.

~~~

Savouries

SAUSAGE ROLLS

Here's where you cheat. Sausage rolls for afternoon tea are tiny, fiddly and too time- consuming to make. Purchase unbaked ones from the supermarket and keep in your freezer until needed. On afternoon tea day, cut each large one into 4 and place these mini-sausage rolls on a greased baking sheet. Brush the top of the pastry with a little milk or beaten egg. Bake at 350° until golden. Serve hot from the oven with a big grin and a garnish of fresh parsley. (Allow 2 or 3 mini-rolls per person.)

CREAM CHEESE AND WATERCRESS SANDWICHES

For each guest:

2 slices bread, 1 white, 1 brown
butter
cream cheese
watercress or, if not in season, alfalfa sprouts
pepper

• Makes 4 small sandwiches per person (2 slices of bread).
• Line up the two slices of bread on top of each other. With a sharp knife, trim the crusts from the slices.
• Butter the slice of white bread.
• Spread cream cheese generously on the brown bread, sprinkle with freshly ground pepper.

- Lay sprigs of washed and dried watercress generously on the cream cheese.
- Top with the white bread. Press down lightly.
- Cut sandwich into 4 diagonally.
- Serve alternating the brown and white sides.

TEA FOR TWO

"There is very little art in making good tea: if the water is boiling and there is no sparing of the fragrant leaf, the beverage will almost invariably be good. The old fashioned plan of allowing one teaspoonful for each cup and one over, is still practised. Warm the teapot with boiling water; let it remain for two or three minutes for the vessel to become thoroughly hot then pour it away. Put in the tea, pour in a cupful of boiling water, close the lid and let it stand for the tea to draw for five to ten minutes; then fill with boiling water to the amount required. Remove the tea leaves before serving."

Mrs Beeton, The Book of Household Management, 1861

Sweets

Tasty squares and scones are quick and easy, so well worth the effort. Make extra scones and freeze them for another time. Some folk like the plain ones, some prefer the fruit scones. Here are recipes for both. Serve with homemade jam and thick whipped cream.

FINISHING TOUCHES

Victoria has some wonderful stores selling table linens, china and accessories for tea tables, but the one we cannot resist is All in Bloom in historic Trounce Alley. Everything in the store has a floral theme, but the pièce de résistance is a blown glass napkin ring that you can fill with water and pop a fresh flower in the little spout at the top – elegantly unusual.

LEMON SQUARES

Light and tangy morsels that never stay around for long.
Makes 16 to 20 squares.

Base
1 cup all-purpose flour
½ cup butter
¼ cup sugar

Topping
1 cup sugar
2 Tbsp all-purpose flour
½ tsp baking powder
¼ tsp salt
2 eggs, lightly beaten
2 tsp grated lemon zest
3 Tbsp lemon juice
sprinkle icing sugar

- Place base ingredients in a food processor. Process until well mixed.
- Press into an 8 by 8 inch cake pan and bake at 325° for 20 minutes or until golden.
- In food processor, place topping sugar, flour, baking powder, salt, eggs, lemon zest and juice. Process until smooth.
- Spread over base and return to 325° oven. Bake for 20 minutes or until nearly set.
- Cool in pan. Dust with icing sugar. Cut into squares.

SILVER AND LACE

QUESTION: Why were silver tea trays always covered with a linen or lace tray cloth?
ANSWER: So that the bottom of the silver teapot didn't scratch and damage the silver tray (or – horror – scratch off the silver plate!).

PLAIN SCONES

Makes 16 scones.

2 cups all-purpose flour
2 Tbsp sugar
4 tsp baking powder
½ tsp salt
⅓ cup butter
1 egg
1 egg yolk
½ cup light cream (approximately)
1 egg white, lightly beaten
sprinkle sugar

- Mix together lightly with a fork flour, sugar, baking powder and salt.
- Rub in butter with tips of fingers until like breadcrumbs.
- In a small bowl lightly beat egg, egg yolk and cream.
- Add liquid all at once, stirring with a fork. It should make a soft sticky dough. Add more cream if necessary.
- Turn onto well-floured board and knead gently 8 to 10 times.
- Cut dough in half, make 2 balls. Roll each ball to ½ inch thick round, cut into 8 triangles.
- Place triangles onto ungreased baking sheet. Brush with beaten egg white and sprinkle with sugar.
- Bake at 425° for 12 to 15 minutes.

CURRANT SCONES

Makes 12 scones.

2¼ cups all-purpose flour
2 Tbsp sugar
2½ tsp baking powder
½ tsp baking soda
½ tsp salt
½ cup cold butter
½ cup currants
1 cup buttermilk
1 egg, lightly beaten

- Sift together in a large bowl flour, sugar, baking powder, baking soda and salt.

- Cut in butter until like coarse crumbs.
- Stir in currants.
- Add buttermilk all at once, mix with a fork to make a soft sticky dough. Don't overwork.
- Flour hands, gather dough together and turn out onto floured board.
- Knead gently 10 times.
- Pat dough to ¾ inch thick. Cut out scone rounds. Place on an un-greased baking sheet and brush with beaten egg.
- Bake at 425° for 12 to 15 minutes or until golden.

ALMOST INSTANT JAM OF ALMOST ANY KIND

Scones and homemade jam go together like . . . peaches and cream! But Lotusland attracts a stream of constant visitors, and who has time to make jam when in the throes of juggling beds, meals, guests (and books)? We'd given up, then we were given this recipe by a busy friend who runs a Bed and Breakfast. It's impressive. Andrea had a pot of fresh jam on the table for breakfast before Dave had finished scrambling the eggs and making toast.

Makes 1 small jar of jam.

2 cups soft fruit, chopped, if necessary
1 cup sugar
1 sterilized warm small jar
melted wax, if not eating jam immediately

- Place the fruit in a large bowl, cover with plastic wrap. Microwave on high for 5 minutes.
- Remove wrap and discard. Add sugar and stir well. Microwave on high for 5 minutes.
- Stir well again. Microwave for 5 more minutes.
- Test jam by dropping a little from the spoon into a saucer. Run the spoon through it. If the jam puckers, it's ready.
- If jam doesn't pucker, scrape back into bowl and microwave for a further 2 minutes. Try pucker test again.
- Cook in 2-minute units until ready, but DON'T OVERCOOK or you'll get glue.
- Pour finished jam into sterilized jar. Cover with melted wax if not using immediately.

NOTE: *We've made this successfully with strawberries, golden plums, raspberries, blueberries and blackberries. You may need to cook jam as long as 15 minutes if the fruit you've chosen is low in pectin.*

VICTORIA SANDWICH

The classic sponge layer cake that's synonymous with afternoon tea. For an unusual twist, try the floral suggestion on page 153. For a successful light high sponge it is worth buying a small bag of special cake flour.
Makes one 8 inch cake that cuts into 12 slices.

1 cup butter
1 cup sugar
1¾ cups cake flour
4 eggs
2 tsp baking powder
½ tsp salt
1½ tsp vanilla
¼ cup raspberry jam
icing sugar

- Butter two 8 inch round cake pans. Line bottoms with waxed paper, butter again.
- Beat butter until creamy. Beat in sugar until pale and fluffy.
- Sift together flour, baking powder and salt.
- Sprinkle creamed mixture with a quarter of the flour, beat until well blended.
- Beat in 1 egg until well blended. Repeat process, alternating flour and eggs.
- Beat in the vanilla.
- Divide mixture between the 2 prepared pans. Spread evenly, then make a shallow indentation in the centres to help cakes rise flat.
- Bake at 375° for 20 to 25 minutes until cakes are golden, firm to the touch and pull away from the sides of the pans.
- Turn out onto wire racks, remove paper and let cool completely.
- Sandwich together with raspberry jam (if jam is too thick to spread easily, thin with a little fruit liqueur).
- Dust cake top with icing sugar.
- For a special effect, before dusting with icing sugar, lay a decorative paper doily on top of cake, then thickly dust with sugar. Carefully lift off doily and the sugar will be in a lacy pattern.

∼

A Scottish Castle in the
Not-So-Wild West

Another tourist attraction where afternoon tea has figured prominently in its past is Craigdarroch Castle. Built by coal baron Robert Dunsmuir in the 1880s, Craigdarroch was the result of a promise Dunsmuir made to his wife — that if she accompanied him to the far side of the world he would build her a Scottish castle. The resulting edifice has (like the family itself) had its ups and downs, but is now restored to much of its original excessive magnificence. The oak woodwork and the stained glass windows are spectacular and show incredible workmanship. In fact, they alone are worth the entrance fee. If you hike to the very top of the oak stairs you will find a small room. This is where Mrs. Dunsmuir took her tea, looking out over her husband's empire — the railway that connected the shipyard at Esquimalt to the coalfields in Nanaimo on which the Dunsmuir fortune was based. Despite the accounts of the balls, the musical afternoons and spectacular weddings (would you believe twenty-seven bridesmaids and flower girls at one wedding?) held at Craigdarroch, specific food is not often mentioned, though some admiring accounts remain of the amount of alcoholic refreshments consumed. However, we could not conceive of such a determinedly Scottish family not enjoying the following two recipes.

SCOTTISH SHORTBREAD

This genuine Scottish recipe calls for castor sugar, a finer sugar than granulated. Before making the shortbread, pour the measured amount of granulated sugar into the food processor while it's working and process for a few seconds. This will give the fine "melt in the mouth" texture of true shortbread.

Makes 24 slices.

4 cups all-purpose flour
2 cups butter
1 cup castor sugar
   or granulated sugar
1½ cups cornstarch
sprinkle sugar

- Process all ingredients in food processor until just mixed.
- Spread in 3 foil pie pans.
- Bake at 325° for 30 minutes.
- Remove from oven. Turn heat down to 200°.
- Cut shortbread into small wedges, sprinkle with sugar.
- Return to oven and cook at 200° for 30 minutes.
- Cool before separating.
- If preferred, use square pans and cut into fingers.

DUNDEE CAKE

To Scots, this cake with its crown of almonds holds the same pride of place that Victoria Sandwich does for the English.

1½ cups golden raisins
1½ cups currants
⅓ cup candied cherries, halved
⅓ cup candied orange peel
1 tsp grated orange zest
1 tsp grated lemon zest
2 Tbsp lemon juice
¾ cup butter
¾ cup granulated sugar
½ cup almonds, ground
2 cups cake flour, sifted
4 eggs
1 tsp baking powder
¼ tsp salt
½ cup blanched almonds, halved
1 Tbsp milk sweetened with 1 tsp sugar

- Butter, line bottom and butter again a cake pan 8 inches in diameter and 3 inches deep.
- Mix together raisins, currants, candied cherries, orange peel, orange zest, lemon zest and lemon juice. Set aside.
- In a large mixing bowl, beat butter and sugar until creamy, fluffy and pale lemon in colour.
- Stir together the ground almonds and ¼ cup of the flour. Sprinkle ¼ of this mixture over butter mixture and beat well. Beat in 1 egg. Repeat alternately with almond mixture and eggs until all combined.

- Sift together the remaining flour, baking powder and salt, and fold into the batter.
- Gently stir in the reserved fruit. Mix well.
- Turn into prepared pan and level with a spatula.
- Arrange 4 split almonds, flat side down, in a cross at the cake's centre. Arrange the other almonds in two concentric circles.
- Bake at 300° for 1 hour and 15 minutes.
- Brush cake surface with the sweetened milk. Bake for 30 to 45 minutes longer or until a cake tester comes out clean.
- Cool cake pan on a wire rack for 30 minutes before turning out. Remove paper and cool completely.
- Wrap cake in plastic and store in an airtight tin for at least 24 hours (and preferably a week) before serving, to allow it to age and moisten and the flavour to fully develop.
- Serve in small slices with tea.

ᕗ

Craigflower Manor and Schoolhouse

Craigflower Manor and Schoolhouse in Esquimalt are all that remain of a set of four farms that serviced the Hudson's Bay fort. Once the H.B.C. fort was established, it was imperative to have supplies produced on the spot as soon as possible, rather than importing them. Craigflower grew not only vegetables and fruit, but also provided beef, flour and sawn lumber to the surrounding community. By the end of 1854 the enterprising Mr. Mackenzie of Craigflower was employing so many families that there were thirty children under the age of fifteen, so a schoolhouse was built. Situated on opposite sides of the scenic Gorge (the children crossed to school in a boat), these buildings are now preserved as heritage sites and are delightful tourist destinations. Between Craigflower, Point Ellice and the Carr Residence, we get a fantastic picture of how food was prepared in the past. Watch for some of the incredible household gadgets and try to figure out how they were used. Sometimes even the guides aren't sure!

STEAK AND KIDNEY PIE

Craigflower Farm produced beef and had its own slaughterhouse. Offal was not discarded, nor disdained as second-class meat. Kidneys, in fact, were a treat, and this combination has remained one of the great gourmet dishes of the much-maligned food from the British Isles.

Serves 8.

½ recipe Never-fail Pastry *(see page 48)*

Filling

This needs to be cooled before covering with pastry, so could be made the day before.

2 lbs stewing beef, trimmed of fat and cubed
⅓ cup flour
¼ cup vegetable oil
2 onions, chopped
2 garlic cloves, minced
1 lb beef kidney, fat and membrane removed
1 cup beef stock or water
2 cups beer
1 Tbsp Worcestershire sauce
½ tsp dried rosemary
½ tsp dried oregano
1 bay leaf
2 tsp salt
pepper
1 cup carrots, sliced
½ lb mushrooms, washed and sliced
1 egg, slightly beaten

- Dredge cubed beef with flour.
- Heat oil in bottom of Dutch oven, add the onions and garlic and sauté until transparent. Remove with slotted spoon and reserve.
- Add floured meat and cook until browned on all sides.
- Thinly slice the trimmed kidney (remove any centre core) and add to the browning meat, tossing gently for 3 minutes.
- Return the onions and garlic to the pot. Add the stock, beer, spices, carrots and mushrooms. Bring to the boil and stir until sauce is smooth and thickened.
- Cover and simmer for 1 to 1½ hours or until meat is tender.

(Check halfway and add a little more beer or water if necessary.) Stir occasionally.
- Check seasoning and adjust as necessary.
- Pour into a deep pie dish or an 11 by 9 inch glass dish and cool.
- Roll out pastry and fit over baking dish. Vent two or three times, brush with egg and bake at 400° for 40 minutes or until pastry is golden and sauce bubbling.

THREE FRUIT PIE

A delicious and unusual combination of two fruits grown in the Craigflower orchard, and dried apricots.

½ recipe Never-fail Pastry *(see page 48)*

Filling

3 ripe pears
3 tart apples
¾ cup dried apricots
⅔ cup sugar
3 Tbsp flour
3 Tbsp butter, cubed
2 Tbsp lemon juice
1 tsp cinnamon
1 tsp ginger
pinch nutmeg
1 egg, lightly beaten
1 tsp sugar

- Peel the apples and pears, halve and core them, and slice into a bowl.
- Cut apricot in half and add to bowl.
- Combine fruit with ⅔ cup sugar, lemon juice, flour and spices.
- Divide pastry in half and pat into 2 balls. Roll out first ball to fit a 10 inch pie plate. Roll out second ball ready to make top.
- Place fruit mixture in pastry case, dot with the cubed butter. Cover with reserved pastry, sealing and crimping the edges well.
- Use any pastry trimmings to make decorative leaves on top. Make a steam vent in the middle.
- Brush pastry with beaten egg, Sprinkle with 1 teaspoon sugar.
- Bake at preheated 425° for 15 minutes. Reduce heat to 350° and

bake for a further 45 minutes.
- After 30 minutes check pie and if it's browning too quickly cover loosely with foil.
- Cool for 30 minutes before serving.

The Carr Residence

How times change. Richard Carr, father of artist and writer Emily Carr, was totally disparaging of any roast of meat less than twenty pounds, dismissing it as "not worth bothering with." The Carr Residence on Government Street in James Bay had a special tin oven that tucked into the fireplace for roasting meat. This oven was brought over at great expense from England, for Carr didn't believe in the new "enclosed ovens." As far as he was concerned, the only way to "roast" meat was literally that, on a spit over a fire. The roast of choice in the Carr household was saddle of mutton (as long as it was over twenty pounds). It was cooked on Saturday and eaten cold on Sunday, accompanied by pickled cabbage, potato salad and red currant jelly, and followed by deep dish apple pie with Devonshire cream. Note that all the Sunday's dishes were cold. Richard Carr was devout and no work was done in his house on Sundays.

ROAST LEG OF LAMB

The strong taste of mutton has gone out of favour these days, except for use in stews and curries, and most people prefer their lamb roast hot. Though many people buy lamb in the supermarket, beautiful spring lamb is still produced locally. Two of the nearby Gulf Islands, Saturna and Salt Spring, are famous for their lamb, and it can be ordered directly from farms there.

1 leg of lamb
4 garlic cloves
several sprigs of fresh rosemary
garlic salt
pepper

- Wash and dry leg of lamb.
- Loosen the skin and slip small sprigs of rosemary between the skin and flesh. (If fresh rosemary is unavailable, sprinkle dried rosemary

over the skin with the garlic salt.)
- Cut the garlic cloves into slivers. Make vertical slits through the skin into the meat and insert the slivers.
- Sprinkle leg with garlic, salt and pepper.
- Roast for 20 minutes per pound at 325°.
- Serve with roast potatoes, fresh garden peas tossed in a little butter, and lots of fresh chopped mint.

VICTORIANS AND FOOD: EMILY CARR

She was a genius. Her paintings and writings conveyed the soul of the west coast in a form years ahead of her time. But her way of life and eccentricities so offended Victoria's society that only in the last few years has Victoria felt comfortable truly acknowledging her. Tales of her pushing her pet monkey around in a baby carriage shocked her neighbours. People hated her cutting remarks, such as "had a dull dinner with a dull woman at the dull Empress." Emily herself hated guests and often resented the time that had to be given to cooking. "I gave a birthday dinner party. Of the four guests one was a vegetarian, one a diabetic, one treating for biliousness and the remaining one a straightforward eater. I cooked all afternoon but I hated the foodstuffs as I dished up the messes . . . ." All this, combined with her odd furniture arrangements of chairs hanging from the ceiling to be lowered by pulleys when guests arrived, conspired to make her an embarrassment to a society that liked to surround itself with conventions and proprieties more British than Britain.

Fortunately, time heals. Her birthplace, the Carr Residence, is now open to the public; some of her paintings can be seen in Art Gallery of Greater Victoria in Rockland; and a gallery named after her was created on Wharf Street in what was her father's warehouse, though the gallery is now closed. Emily Carr's books can be now be purchased at almost every bookstore, and our personal favourite, The House of All Sorts tells of her attempt to run a boarding house in the James Bay area.

After years of neglect Emily can finally take a public bow.

FATLESS ROAST POTATOES

Roast potatoes cooked in the meat fat are a favourite that many of us try not to eat. Here's a way that sidesteps the fat and makes them taste almost as good.

- Peel and parboil potatoes in saltless water.
- Drain off water and replace open saucepan over the residual heat for a few seconds to steam the last of the water from the potatoes.
- Remove from heat. Place lid on saucepan and shake pan vigorously up and down for a few seconds, to fluff up the surfaces of the potatoes.
- Tip potatoes onto a baking sheet (sprinkle with a little salt, if you wish) and roast in oven for 30 minutes at 325° or until crisp and golden brown.

DEEP DISH APPLE PIE

Emily Carr tells us she had this every Sunday in her youth, but doesn't tell us exactly what she means by the term "deep dish." Some recipes use the term to refer to a deep two-crust pie, others to a one-crust top over a deep filling and yet another to a deep apple filling with an oatmeal crumb crust. We have decided to present you with a delicious apple filling that can be used with a pie crust or oatmeal crumb topping, or even served on its own as a cold compote to cut down on calories.
Serves 4 to 6.

1 lemon, zest and juice
1 orange, zest and juice
extra orange juice to make 1 cup of liquid
6 medium sour apples, peeled, cored and sliced
½ cup sugar

- Peel zest from lemon and orange, reserve.
- Squeeze juice from lemon and orange, make up to 1 cup with extra orange juice.
- Prepare apples and place in a saucepan.
- Pour juice over apples and stir so all surfaces are covered (work quickly to prevent apples from browning). Stir in fruit zest and sugar.
- Bring to the boil, reduce heat immediately and simmer until syrup is slightly thickened and apples are just soft. Stir occasionally and taste-check for sugar content; add extra if needed, or a little more juice if the syrup seems to be too thick. (It should be thick enough to mound on a spoon.)
- Use in pies, serve hot or cold with cream or ice cream, or freeze to use later.

Raspberry Mousse

Dunsmuir's imposing Craigdarroch Castle was the scene of many elaborate meals

VICTORIANS AND FOOD: MISS WILSON
& LOUIS THE LUSH

Miss Victoria Jane Wilson was a hermit known for her beautiful chateau and gardens that no one was allowed to see, her immaculate appearance and her closets full of clothes she never wore. (After her death in 1949, a hundred pairs of unworn gloves were put up for auction.) She raised eyebrows in 1909 by purchasing a top-of-the-line electric brougham for $7,000, but by the time of her death it had driven only forty-five miles and had one charge on its battery. Many tales are told of her eccentricities, but she was best known for willing her estate to her faithful companion "Louis the Lush" for the duration of his lifetime. Louis was a South American macaw.

Yue Wah Wong, Miss Wilson's Chinese gardener, was hired to look after Louis, and Louis thrived on a diet of brandy, walnuts, almonds, apples and hard-boiled eggs. After Wong's death in 1966, events got a little hazy, with the parrot reportedly being moved to a secret location to prevent kidnapping or worse! However, it is said upon good authority that Louis is now reunited with his mistress, and the restive heirs received their long overdue money.

Miss Wilson's chateau was demolished and the hotel Chateau Victoria built on the site. The lounge still bears her name, Victoria Jane's, and the penthouse restaurant is called The Parrot House in memory of "Louis the Lush."

NUT CHOCOLATE FONDUE
(or BIRDIE NUM NUMS)

Finding a recipe featuring Louis the Lush's list of ingredients was a challenge, but Nut Chocolate Fondue matches pretty well. (The hard-boiled egg is optional.)
Serves 4 to 6.

1 lb semi-sweet chocolate
1 cup whipping cream
¼ cup brandy
1 cup walnuts or almonds, crushed
1 plateful fresh fruit:
apple slices
orange segments

strawberries
banana chunks
kiwi slices
pineapple chunks

- Chop the chocolate and melt in a double saucepan over low heat.
- Stir in the cream and brandy. Keep stirring until combined and warm.
- Stir in the chopped nuts.
- Serve in a ceramic fondue pot with a tea light underneath to keep the chocolate warm.
- Place the fruit plate in the middle. Guests dip the fruit in the sauce with long forks (or beaks).

7

Waterfront City

The ocean surrounding Vancouver Island is both admired and cursed. There is nothing more romantic than a colourful sunset, or moonlight, reflecting on the waves; nothing more idyllic than basking in the sun on a headland and watching the water sparkle below; nothing more awe-inspiring than watching the winter breakers assault the Dallas Road causeway. There is also nothing more irritating than waiting in long ferry lineups on a hot summer day when trying to get to (or from) the mainland.

Victorians live on an island – a big one, to be sure, but still an island. It separates and disconnects us from what goes on in the rest of Canada, so we have a different relationship to our country. It also means that the ocean is not just something pretty to look at, the ocean is our highway, our protecting wall and a vital resource.

Drive over the Johnson Street bridge and take the first right to Ocean Pointe (there are places with two hours' free parking). Stroll down the walk built along the Songhees Peninsula waterfront and watch the traffic using the Inner Harbour. It's incredibly busy. Several large ferries regularly negotiate the awkward entrance, pleasure boats zip past and weave in and out among the more sedate fishing boats. You'll see trawlers and Coast Guard vessels, and a variety of cargo ships, tugs and barges, canoes, kayaks and zodiacs, interspersed with the little harbour ferries chugging around. Among them all, float planes are frequently landing and taking off.

The view most people see is from the Empress. It's pretty, lots of interesting visitors enjoying the excitement of an attractive marina full of sleek boats. The causeway is also home to pavement artists and portrait painters, interspersed with buskers ranging from string quartets, to bagpipers to rock musicians. The view from Songhees is different. Here you are in no doubt that this is a working port, the real heart of Victoria. You'll see shipping from around the Pacific bearing supplies to be unloaded at docks on the west side of the harbour and further up the Gorge. You notice customs buildings and inspection sheds, warehouses, docks and derricks. Ships come for servicing in the dry docks on the other side of Johnson Street, and if you're lucky you will see the bridge go up to let a large marine vessel enter the Gorge area.

From Ocean Pointe you can look across to the Inner Harbour and see the ghost of the old city looking back at you much as it did in the early days. Old business frontages look seaward along Wharf Street, interspersed with ship chandlers and warehouses. You are too far away to see that they now masquerade as restaurants and boutiques, so the image remains almost complete.

Listen; you are too far away from town to hear the city bustle, so the bustle of the sea and its traffic assaults your ears, and we mean assault. It's noisy. The throb of ferries and large cargo vessels, the roar of the sea planes and the chugging of smaller craft are punctuated with zooms from passing speed boats, the warning blare from a lighthouse and the screams of gulls fighting over scraps from the fish boats.

Yes, Victoria is a port, and it's worth exploring.

~~~

A Restaurant Not Quite Afloat

Start your visit at the Princess Mary Restaurant on Harbour Road, just across the Johnson Street bridge. The Princess Mary was a well-known coastal steamer that plied the waters on several routes around Vancouver Island, including the Gulf Islands and across to Powell River. During the twenties and thirties she was renowned for her "Around Vancouver Island Week-long Cruise," $60 including berth and meals. Her dining room had a reputation for elegance and good food. She was retired in the fifties and her hull sold as a barge. But her cafeteria and dining room were salvaged and carefully rebuilt on the docks where she now flourishes as the Princess Mary Restaurant, renowned for her Manhattan clam chowder. As might be expected, seafood is a specialty here, but leave room for the desserts.

CLAM CHOWDER

Not the Princess Mary's recipe, but just as delicious.
Serves 6 to 8.

6 slices bacon, cut into ½ inch pieces
1 onion, sliced
1 garlic clove, chopped
4 cups potatoes, cooked and cut into cubes
3 cups clams, drained (save liquid)
4 cups half-and-half cream
1 tsp salt
½ tsp pepper
½ tsp garlic salt
4 Tbsp butter
2 tsp cornstarch
1 cup clam liquid

- Fry bacon in large heavy pot until cooked but not crisp.
- Add onions and garlic, cook until soft.
- Add all ingredients except cornstarch and clam liquid, lower heat and cook gently for 5 to 10 minutes until heated through. Do not boil.
- Mix the clam liquid into the cornstarch. Add in a steady stream to the chowder, stirring until thickened.
- Serve immediately.

NOTE: *The clam liquid has a tendency to curdle milk, so always add it last and serve immediately.*

HARBOUR FERRIES

The little harbour ferries are not only cute, but practical. If you wish to go from one side of the harbour to the other, or take a trip up the Gorge, this is the way to do it. In fact, in summer we tend to park our car over on Songhees and hop on the ferry to the Inner Harbour when we have business downtown. This saves the hassle of traffic congestion and, at a couple of dollars or so for the scenic trip, is a bargain. Here's an interesting lunch suggestion. Head to the Inner Harbour and catch the ferry going to Fisherman's Wharf for fresh fish and chips at Barb's Place – wonder if it should be "plaice". Somehow they taste best when eaten wharfside.

BAKED ROCK COD WITH FLAKED CRAB

Rock cod is often caught off the wharfs by weekend fishers. Many throw it back, not realizing it's edible. However, the tough skin excretes some body wastes, so this fish needs immediate skinning and filleting. Once prepared, the flesh is firm and tasty. All the Inner Harbour marinas have cleaning stations, usually with a harbour seal in attendance to snap up scraps tossed into the water. Serves 4.

2 lbs rock cod fillets
4 Tbsp butter
salt and pepper
½ cup green onions, chopped
1 cup tomatoes, chopped and skinned
½ cup dry white wine
¾ cup cooked crabmeat

- Melt the butter in an oven-proof casserole.
- Add the rock cod fillets and sprinkle with salt and pepper.
- Add onions, tomatoes and pour in the wine.
- Flake the crabmeat over the top.
- Bake at 350° for 15 minutes or until fish is firm and white.

RED TIDE

Clam digging sounds like a fun activity (unless you are a clam). Unfortunately, red tide sometimes appears around these coasts without warning, particularly in the summer. It is caused by a bloom of tiny algae, called dinoflagellates, which are sometimes so abundant as to colour the water. They are ingested by clams and produce toxins which may make them unsafe to eat. Although signs are put up on docks, they may not be in evidence early in an outbreak. So don't dig for clams unless you've checked. Red tide is deadly to humans but does not attack the clams and mussels it affects, so they look fine. (Crabs have a different type of digestive system and are not affected.) If you want to be sure you are safe, buy your clams and mussels from the fish markets.

SHELLFISH BOUILLABAISSE

If you're looking for an interesting place to buy fresh seafood, several boats at Fisherman's Wharf usually have crabs. You can also occasionally find a boat selling prawns, and just past Barb's Place there is a fresh fish shop. Open in the summer months only, this is the place you'll find shrimp, mussels, snapper and other denizens of the deep. We were spoilt for choice, so our answer – bouillabaisse.

First, make fish stock:
2 heads and trimmings of white fish
1 carrot, washed and sliced
2 onions, sliced
1 bay leaf
2 white peppercorns
water or wine to cover

- Wash fish debris, discard any discoloured skin.
- Combine all ingredients in a large enameled pot. Bring to the boil and simmer for 1 hour. Strain.

Bouillabaisse
Serves 4.

2 cups fish stock, strained
3 Tbsp olive oil
1 onion, chopped
½ cup celery, chopped
1 garlic clove, minced
pinch rosemary
2 Tbsp parsley, chopped
3 ozs lobster meat, raw
3 ozs scallops, raw
4 ozs prawns, raw
2 ozs crab claw meat
4 ozs clams, raw
2 Tbsp dry sherry
1 cup tomato, skinned and chopped
½ lemon, thinly sliced
1 Tbsp sugar
2 Tbsp salt
¼ tsp cayenne pepper
¾ tsp saffron

- Place olive oil in heavy pan. Add onions, celery, garlic, parsley, rosemary; sauté for 5 minutes or until onions are transparent.
- Add all shellfish and sherry and simmer for 5 minutes.
- Add fish stock and all other ingredients except saffron. Cook on low heat for 10 minutes.
- Stir in saffron and serve with hot fresh bread.

Houseboats and Herbs

Not far from Fisherman's Wharf is "Finger One," the jetty that is home base for several picturesque houseboats that are so delightfully idiosyncratic they look like the set of the movie *Popeye*. In the summer their small decks and window ledges are chock-a-block with pots of herbs, tomatoes and vegetables, augmented by vivid hanging baskets of flowers. Judging by their obvious green thumbs, houseboat owners love good food.

FRESH TOMATO AND BASIL SAUCE

Here's a recipe featuring a collection of the herbs we saw growing on their decks.

Makes about 5 cups.

3 lbs ripe tomatoes, peeled and chopped
¼ cup olive oil
1 small onion, chopped
3 green onions, chopped, including stems
3 garlic cloves, minced
½ tsp ground black pepper
¼ tsp salt
¼ cup fresh basil, chopped

- In a large saucepan, heat oil and cook onions, green onions and garlic until soft.
- Add tomatoes, salt and pepper. Stir. Bring to the boil, then reduce heat and simmer uncovered for about 20 minutes.
- Stir in basil and simmer for 5 minutes.
- Serve over pasta or couscous.

VICTORIANS AND FOOD: HELENA & ROBERT LABBÉ

Helena and Robert Labbé run Bay Scallops Ltd, the summer fish shop at Fisherman's Wharf. Helena is Portuguese and Robert, French-Canadian, so you can converse in Portuguese, Spanish or French as well as English. The sea is their life as well as livelihood, as not content with selling fish on the wharf, they live on a boat in the marina. They sell fish only and are not licensed to prepare it for consumption in any way. However . . . if you fancy lunching on oysters (raw, that is), this is the place to come. Helena will sell you the oysters, then loan you a knife to shuck them, and even pass over the Tabasco sauce. We supped royally on the dock, tossing the empty shells into the ocean, watched closely by a gull hoping we'd drop a full one, and Helena and Robert's children, who obviously thought we were mad.

How to Get Crabby and Enjoy It

The local crab is plentiful and delicious, and many Victorians have a carefully guarded spot where they drop a crab pot. Crabs can be eaten year-round and are not affected by red tide, but there are limits on the sizes for "keepers." Check the fishing regulations. Incidentally, despite the folk belief, crabs do not scream when dropped in boiling water. We do apologize to them first, though.

FRESH CRAB

- Choose a pot big enough to easily hold the number of crabs to be cooked. (Allow 1 crab per person; pot must be big enough for the water to completely cover the crab.)
- Half fill with water, season with salt and bring to a full boil.
- Drop in live crabs and cook at a rolling boil for 10 minutes.
- Remove crab, pull off back shell and run under cold water immediately, discarding the gut and gills from the hollow of the body cavity.
- You will be left with a "honeycomb" that, like the attached claws and legs, is full of tasty meat.
- The easiest way to eat crabs is to take the crabs and your guests to the nearest beach for a picnic. There everyone can pick and chew

and finally return the shell remnants to the ocean and swill their hands at the same time.

• If you are preparing crabmeat for a recipe, then you have the job of picking out the crabmeat. Fiddly, but here are a couple of recipes that make the effort worthwhile.

CRAB QUICHE

Makes a fabulous West Coast meal when teamed with a garden-fresh Caesar salad and Bubble Bread (see recipe page 52).
Serves 4 to 6.

1 - 8 inch-deep pastry shell, unbaked
2 Dungeness crabs, cooked and meat shucked
1 carrot, grated
1 celery stalk, chopped
4 green onions, chopped
1 cup cheese, grated
½ cup Parmesan cheese
6 eggs, beaten
1 cup milk
salt and pepper

• Cook crabs *(see instructions page 95)*, clean and shuck meat.
• Toss together flaked meat with the carrot, celery, onions and cheeses. Pile into pastry case.
• Lightly beat the eggs and milk with salt and pepper to taste. Pour over the other ingredients.
• Bake at 350° for 40 minutes or until quiche is firm.

CREAMY CRAB AND BASIL PASTA

A great dish for entertaining as the sauce can be made ahead, then warmed and served over the cooked pasta at the last minute.

Sauce
1 Dungeness crab, approximately 2 lbs
2 cups water
½ cup dry white wine
5 ozs small shrimp, cooked and shelled
1 tsp Dijon mustard

2 cups cream
3 Tbsp rice flour
2 Tbsp water
½ cup fresh basil, chopped
6 green onions, chopped
½ red pepper, chopped
salt and pepper

- Boil crab *(see instructions page 95)*, shuck meat, discard guts and gills, but reserve shell. Set meat aside.
- Boil shell in 2 cups of water for 15 minutes. Strain stock and discard shell.
- Add wine to stock and boil until reduced to half.
- Lower heat, stir in crabmeat, shrimp, mustard and cream.
- Blend rice flour with 2 tablespoons water and stir into crab mixture. Stir gently until thickened.
- Adjust seasoning.
- Stir in basil, onions and pepper, heat through and serve over pasta.
- Sauce can be made up to 24 hours ahead if kept in fridge.

Pasta

Serves 4.

1 lb tagliatelli pasta
   or fettuccine
salted boiling water
1 Tbsp cooking oil
2 Tbsp olive oil

- Bring large pot of salted water to boil. Add 1 tablespoon cooking oil. Drop in pasta.
- Cook uncovered until al dente.
- Drain, toss in olive oil.
- Serve topped with crab and basil sauce.

~~~~

Fishing and Whale Watching

The wharfs and marinas serviced by the harbour ferries are the place to find charter boats that will take you salmon fishing or whale and wildlife watching. While the gray whales only migrate off the west coast and are mainly seen in spring and fall, pods of *Orca* (killer whales) can be seen all year round, and a trip up the Gorge will often be enlivened by sightings of otters and seals. If heading out in your own boat and you sight *Orca* or other sea creatures, just throttle back and quietly observe from a distance. Do not hassle the pod, attempt to drive through it or chase any of its members. Note how many *Orca* or whales are sighted and phone in the information to the Whale Sighting and Stranding Report Line when you return to the marina.

TERIYAKI SALMON BARBECUE

A barbecue recipe with a delicious Japanese "toffee" flavour when you want to share a plentiful "catch" with friends.
Serves 6 to 8.

4 to 6 lbs fillet of salmon, with the skin left on
1 cup soya sauce
¼ cup brown sugar, packed
2 garlic cloves, crushed
½ medium onion, diced
2 Tbsp lemon juice
1 tsp grated ginger root

• Lay the fillet in a large dish, skin side up.
• Mix together all ingredients and pour over fish.
• Cover with plastic wrap and marinate overnight.
• Barbecue, skin side down, for approximately 20 minutes or until it flakes easily.

SCALLOP CEVICHE

Although this is a "no cook" dish, you do not eat raw fish. The acidity of the lemon and lime juice has the same effect on the protein content of fish as heat does. The fish is "cooked" in the cold juice. This dish is pretty served in actual scallop shells (try Capitol Iron).

Serves 4.

1 lb scallops, raw
½ cup lemon juice
½ cup lime juice
½ red onion, diced
½ red pepper, diced
1 canned green chili pepper, washed and diced
¼ cup olive oil
3 Tbsp lime juice
1 Tbsp fresh coriander, chopped
1 garlic clove, minced
¼ tsp dried oregano
salt and pepper
4 small butter or red lettuce leaves

- If the scallops are large, cut in half.
- Place scallops in a glass bowl, pour in the lemon and ½ cup of lime juice. Cover and refrigerate for at least 5 hours or overnight (stir occasionally).
- Drain scallops well.
- Stir in all other ingredients except lettuce, seasoning to taste.
- Cover and refrigerate for at least 1 hour.
- Line scallop shells with lettuce, and divide scallop mixture among them.
- Garnish with sprigs of fresh herbs and a lemon twist.

CAPITAL IRON

If you want a feel for an old waterside warehouse, go and poke around Capital Iron on Store Street. Established in 1867, it outwardly has remained a virtually unchanged waterfront feature. Here's where Victorians come for almost any kind of household or cooking needs. Need a special piece of line for fishing? Try Capital Iron's basement. If your barbecue grill has rusted, poke around Capital Iron's scrap yard. You can find all kinds of outdated marine equipment and if you've always wanted an old-fashioned brass diving helmet, this is the place. Make sure you pause to look at the photos on the main floor staircase — shots of sailing ships and steamers that plied the water here, and two panoramas of Victoria, one taken in 1877, the other in 1981 (both showing the store). Most interesting.

~

Symphony Splash

The Inner Harbour is not just known for its boats and fishing; this is the site of Victoria's annual Symphony Splash.

Picture a wonderfully warm August evening. There in the middle of the harbour floats a raft containing the Victoria Symphony Orchestra conducted by the indomitable Peter McCoppin. Thousands of people throng the causeway and wharfs, beg space on boat decks in the marina, lounge on balconies and terraces of overlooking hotels and condominiums, lie on the legislative grounds and listen. The music from what must be the most fantastically scenic free concert anywhere floats over it all. What an experience.

In our opinion there is only one dish that lives up to the challenge.

SIMPLY STRAWBERRIES AND CHAMPAGNE

1 magnum chilled champagne
glasses and ice bucket
1 enormous bowl of fresh strawberries
1 bowl brown sugar
1 bowl sour cream, lightly whipped with a fork
1 set of lawn chairs, preferably on a balcony with a view
   of the harbour
1 coffee table
1 set of close friends

- Wash, dry, but don't hull strawberries; place in bowl on coffee table.
- Flank with bowls of brown sugar and sour cream, champagne bottle and glasses.
- Set chairs within easy reach.
- While listening to music, lazily reach out for a strawberry. Holding firmly by the hull, dip in sour cream, dip in brown sugar and nibble on between sips of champagne.
- Reputed to heighten one's listening powers and certainly heightens one's pleasure.

⌒↝

Seaside Picnics

Not all of Victoria's waterfront is port. Beacon Hill Park runs down to the water on the opposite side of the peninsula from the Inner Harbour. It's a beautiful park, one of the places to see the wild camas lilies in the spring. Here you can picnic, feed ducks, smell roses or wander on the cliff tops and admire the views across the Strait. Beacon Hill is a favourite place for luncheon picnics for staff in nearby government and office buildings. Here's a seaside picnic spread that can be packaged in small dishes and used as a dip for veggies, or spread on sourdough biscuits.

SALMON PÂTÉ

Serves 6 to 8.

1 can (7¾ ozs) salmon, drained
2 Tbsp minced onion
1 garlic clove, chopped
2 Tbsp mayonnaise
½ cup butter, melted
1 Tbsp lemon or lime juice
1 tsp fresh dill
salt and pepper, to taste

• Place all ingredients in a food processor and blend until smooth.
• Pour into several small or one large crock. Chill.
• Garnish with chopped parsley and lemon wedges.
• Will keep for 1 week in fridge.

⌒↝

Scuba Squid

Dusk at the Ogden Point breakwater is the time for strange happenings. Young men and women leap out of cars, wriggle into wet suits and disappear into the dark water. Nighttime is one of the best periods to see some of the sea creatures around the breakwater. Apparently, octopus, a large variety of fish as well as a collection of sea anemones, tube worms and starfish inhabit the cracks below water level. Further out, squid may be seen in the kelp beds. Inquire at the scuba diving clubs for further information.

SAUTÉED CALAMARI (SQUID)

Serves 2 to 3.

2 medium squid, cleaned and cartilage removed
2 Tbsp olive oil
4 large mushrooms, sliced
2 green onions, chopped
1 clove garlic, chopped
1 tomato, peeled and chopped
3 Tbsp sherry
1½ Tbsp lemon juice
parsley, chopped

• Score squid in diamond patterns, then cut into 2 inch strips.
• Heat oil in heavy frypan, add mushrooms, onions and garlic and cook for 2 to 3 minutes or until mushrooms are tender.
• Add squid and tomato, cook gently for 5 to 7 minutes (do not overcook or squid goes rubbery).
• Pour off any oil that's left, add sherry and lemon juice and simmer for 1 minute.
• Serve over rice and sprinkle with chopped parsley.

The Beach Hotels

After driving through Beacon Hill Park, join the scenic Marine Drive and wend your way along the coast to the Oak Bay Beach Hotel. This is the last survivor of several beach hotels that had their heyday in the twenties and thirties. Now hemmed in by condominiums, the hotel retains enough remnants of the old grounds and what was a beachside swimming pool for you to imagine its original elegance. Once situated on spacious grounds and with its own farm to supply all its vegetables, poultry and eggs, the Oak Bay Beach Hotel was a favourite spot for Victorians, especially the locals who gathered for high tea on a regular basis. This tradition has remained and, in fact, the Oak Bay Beach Hotel is a still a favourite watering hole for locals as well as tourists. The current owners have taken advantage of modern trends to augment their status as Victoria's only beach hotel. They offer dinner cruises. You can dress elegantly, walk through the winding garden path to the private dock and step aboard a sleek vessel equipped with

Fresh crab, pasta with Fresh tomato and basil dressing

Four courageous ladies catch crabs in the Esquimalt Lagoon about 1907

an elegant dining room. Enjoy champagne, candlelight and a four-course meal as you cruise though sunset and scenery. What more could one wish for?

TRADITIONAL WEDDING CAKE

Apparently the boat is the place for marriage proposals!

Night Before Cooking

1 cup blanched almonds, slivered
1 lb candied cherries
1 lb mixed peel, chopped
2 cups raisins
1 cup currants
1 cup dates, chopped
1 cup dried apricots, chopped
½ cup brandy

- Combine fruit and almonds in a large bowl, and stir in the brandy.
- Cover with plastic wrap and leave to soak overnight at room temperature.

Next Day

- Grease a large (8 x 8 x 3 inch square or a 9 x 3 inch round) cake pan, and line bottom and sides with 2 layers of baking parchment or brown paper. Grease again.
- Preheat oven to 275°.

1 cup butter
2 cups brown sugar
6 eggs
2½ cups all-purpose flour
½ tsp baking soda
1 tsp cloves
1 tsp allspice
1 tsp ginger
1 tsp cinnamon
½ tsp salt
¾ cup light molasses
¾ cup apple juice

- Dredge soaked fruit with ½ cup of the flour and set aside.

- Cream the butter, gradually adding the brown sugar until light and fluffy.
- Beat in the the eggs one at a time.
- Sift together the remaining flour and all the dry ingredients.
- Mix together the apple juice and molasses.
- Alternately add the dry ingredients and the liquid ingredients to the egg mixture, making 4 dry and 3 liquid additions. Mix until the flour is absorbed. There may be be a few lumps.
- Fold in the fruit.
- Bake at 275° for 3½ to 4 hours or until tests done.
- Turn out of pan and carefully peel off the paper.
- Cool completely.
- Wrap well in plastic wrap and seal in a plastic bag or an airtight tin. Store on the shelf in a cool dark place for a minimum of 6 weeks. It will keep almost indefinitely.
- This cake should be coated with almond paste and iced with royal icing for weddings. However, it is so rich and delicious on its own that we use it as our Christmas cake, slicing and serving it as is.

8

Maritime City

Douglas chose the site of Victoria primarily for its level building site and adjacent agricultural land, and he recognized that its convoluted harbour entrance was a drawback. The British Navy thought Victoria was a ridiculous choice. They had other needs, essentially a deeper and more easily negotiated harbour entrance, so chose a bay three miles to the west, one the Spanish Navy had used many years earlier. Now known as Esquimalt, this bay has become Canada's second largest naval port.

Esquimalt is another name that's food related – or do we mean drink related? Taken from the aboriginal phrase *Is-whoy-malth*, meaning the "place of gently shoaling water," the name refers to the most vital spot in the large bay, the place where the First Nations got their fresh drinking water, a shallow flat near the mouth of Mill Stream. The British Navy used the same spot to refill its water casks before returning to sea. Currently the Canadian Navy at Esquimalt provisions its ships utilizing the surrounding city as a gigantic support system, continuing the tradition of mutual support that began with the earliest contact.

The combined activities of Esquimalt and Victoria make up a port with an incredibly complex and varied maritime history.

Port Victoria today is a tourist attraction, but is reasonably staid. The last time anything dramatic hit the headlines was when the populace lined the breakwater to wave goodbye to the destroyers heading out from Esquimalt to the Gulf War, and again to welcome them safely back.

Staid Victoria has a colourful past. Whalers, sealers and rumrunners have all pursued their various trades from the docks. There were raids for liquor and raids for opium, and dockside rumours were wild and exciting. Fish boats once tied up alongside early immigrant ships travelling round the Horn, and later shared the harbour with the magnificent Canadian Pacific Empress liners that visited Victoria providing world tours for the wealthy. Now the fishing boats tie up alongside pleasure craft and adjacent to the modern ferries which shuttle tourists across the Juan de Fuca Strait from Victoria to the U.S.A. The harbour doesn't have quite the same excitement, but it remembers a rich past.

The Spaniards Take Possession

The first non-Native visitors here were the Spanish. In 1790 they sailed into what is now Esquimalt Harbour, came ashore and planted a cross to take possession of the area, naming the bay *Puerto de Cordova*. They were intrepid explorers and though supplied with what Captain Cook described as "small and poorly equipt ships," explored up and down the coast for several years. Eventually, after some argument around the Nootka Treaty, Spain gave up its claim on this area and left.

SPANISH RICE

Spanish names still remain in the region to hint at the breadth of exploration done by Spanish galleons navigating these waters, among them Galiano, Saturna, Cortes and Quadra islands, Juan de Fuca Strait and, in the Victoria area, Cordova Bay and Gonzales Point. Think of their intrepid voyages while enjoying this tasty entrée, perhaps with a gutsy Spanish red vino.
    Serves 4 to 6.

    6 slices bacon
    2 cups rice, uncooked
    1 cup onion, sliced
    2½ cups canned tomatoes, chopped
    1 tsp salt
    2 tsp paprika
    3 garlic cloves, chopped
    1 green pepper, chopped
    1 red pepper, chopped

- In a large frying pan, cook bacon until crisp. Drain and crumble. Reserve dripping in pan.
- Add rice to bacon dripping and fry until golden.
- Add onions. Sauté until brown.
- Add bacon, chopped tomatoes, salt, paprika, garlic and peppers. Stir well.
- Steam mixture in a double boiler for about 1 hour. Stir regularly.
- Serve hot.

Cooking with Cook

One of the best-known explorers is that seaman extraordinary Captain James Cook. He sailed just about everywhere — except Victoria — and made Britain's first landfall on the B.C. coast at Nootka in 1779. Although he missed the site of Victoria, Victorians have not missed him, for he is remembered by a statue on the causeway in front of the Empress Hotel. (Dave nods to a fellow Yorkshireman every time he passes by.) Captain Cook has a permanent place in food history, as he was the first captain who insisted on his men eating fresh vegetables and thus made the first progress against deaths from scurvy, a vitamin C deficiency disease.

YORKSHIRE HERRING PIE

Hailing from Whitby, Yorkshire, Cook must have eaten the following dish many times. It is occasionally known as Captain Cook Pie. It can also be made with cod or mackerel fillets.
Serves 6.

6 fresh herring fillets
2 cups cold water, salted
6 medium potatoes
3 tart apples
1 onion, sliced
1 tsp fresh parsley, chopped
2 Tbsp butter
1 cup beer
salt and pepper, to taste

- Cut each herring fillet into three and soak in salted water for 20 minutes. Drain.
- Peel and parboil the potatoes, drain and slice thinly.
- Peel, core and slice the apples.
- Grease an ovenproof casserole dish, line with sliced potatoes, then a layer of apple slices and then some onion.
- Sprinkle with salt and pepper.
- Add a layer of herring fillets and sprinkle with parsley.
- Repeat layers until all ingredients have been used, finishing with a layer of potatoes.
- Add the beer, and dot with butter.
- Cover casserole and bake at 350° for 45 minutes.
- Remove lid and bake uncovered for a further 15 minutes or until potatoes are soft and browned on top.
- Traditionally, this dish is served with pickled red cabbage.

Salmon for Breakfast

After James Douglas built Fort Victoria, the British Navy naturally came to call. In 1845, HMS America brought a distinguished visitor: Captain John Gordon, who was gathering data to resolve the boundary dispute between Britain and the United States over the Oregon Territory. Captain Gordon was taken to Victoria by launch, where he was delighted to be served salmon for breakfast. Being a traditional Scot, he asked to go out salmon fishing, but was horrified to find the salmon caught by bait and line instead of with a fly in the Scottish manner. He thought it was "an awfu' way to catch salmon." When the British government abandoned Oregon, it was said the decision was made because the salmon here "did not know enough to take the fly."

SCRAMBLED EGGS WITH SMOKED SALMON

We often enjoy salmon for breakfast, and this dish is a fast favourite of our Bed and Breakfast guests.
Serves 4 to 6.

12 eggs
1 cup milk
1 tsp fresh dill
salt and pepper, to taste
½ lb smoked salmon, chopped
1 tsp butter

- Gently melt butter in saucepan. Tip across bottom and around sides until coated.
- Beat eggs until frothy, add milk, dill and seasonings and beat well.
- Pour into saucepan and cook over low heat, stirring gently until thickened but still creamy.
- Stir in chopped smoked salmon and gently mix through.
- Serve on toast, hot fresh bannock or toasted buttered crumpet.

The Navy and the Ladies

The British Navy really arrived when, in 1848, HMS *Constance* sailed into Esquimalt Harbour and made it her base. Naturally, there was formal contact between the Navy and the fort, and invitations to dinners and receptions were exchanged.

Unfortunately, the three-mile distance between the fort and Esquimalt proved a severe obstacle to socializing. At first trips were by sea, but a storm caused the loss of a small boat, an officer and two seamen. Another party lost its way in the woods on the way to the fort, and even though Douglas provided a guide for the return journey, the group ended up in a ditch in the dark. In 1852 the Navy slashed a road through the forest. This connected not only the naval base, but also Craigflower Farm, and a sawmill and gristmill on the Esquimalt Harbour, to Victoria.

With the road, officials of the fort and surrounding settlement — and their wives and daughters — became readily accessible to the naval officers, whose visits relieved the social tedium and added a somewhat exotic element to the Victoria establishment. Not to be outdone, the officers held dinners and dances onboard ship. One young lady told an officer how glad she was to see him, but he was disconcerted when she explained that it was not so much because of his personal attractiveness, but because the governor provided fresh beef more frequently when the Navy was in. Not all officers got the cold shoulder; in due course, some of them found wives in this remote outpost of the Empire.

WARDROOM STYLE KIDNEYS

The ladies might have been entertained with a version of this elegant dish from navy tradition.
Serves 4.

2 beef kidneys
1 Tbsp oil
2 Tbsp butter
2 Tbsp cream
salt and pepper
8 medium mushrooms, thickly sliced
1 bay leaf
pinch ground cloves
2 Tbsp Plymouth gin

- Cut kidneys in half lengthwise and trim off fatty core and other fat.
- Season with salt and pepper and sprinkle with the ground cloves.
- Heat the oil in a frying pan and add the butter when hot.
- Crumple and add the bay leaf.
- Add kidneys and sauté quickly, turning frequently until pink in the middle.
- Add mushrooms and let them soften.
- Pour off any fat and scrape down the sides.
- Pour gin over, ignite, then put out flames with pan lid.
- Add cream and blend with sauce.
- Taste for seasoning, reheat but do not boil.
- Serve over toast.

The Finest Admiral?

Until recent years, a rum ration, nicknamed grog, was regarded as necessary to Navy life, but after long voyages the essential supplies sometimes ran short. When the officers brought their thirsts down the road to Victoria, the equally dry ordinary seamen followed, and contributed greatly to the success of new drinking and whoring establishments that sprang up along Johnson Street. Officers and men alike found the return journey more difficult.

On one occasion, after a picnic on Beacon Hill, a drunken bagpiper led his equally lubricated companions off to Esquimalt. The journey took a long time, not only because the piper kept falling down, but because in the darkness they took Donald Macauley's bull to be a grizzly bear.

Macauley himself was bailiff of the Viewfield Farm, and was not above taking a dram on suitable occasions. One such was another picnic, this time hosted by Admiral Fairfax Moresby. When the admiral offered Macauley a glass of wine, the Scot announced solemnly, "Sir, you are the finest admiral I ever did see." Unfortunately, he spoiled the effect by adding (perhaps with a hiccup), "You are the first admiral I ever did see."

LEMON AND RUM CAKE

To enjoy a naval tradition in more nourishing form, try our favourite rum cake. But don't drive after eating it.

Cake
1 pkg (510 gm) golden cake mix
1 pkg (4 servings) instant lemon pudding
2 eggs
½ cup rum
½ cup oil
½ cup water
1 tsp lemon flavouring

Sauce
⅓ cup rum
⅓ cup butter
½ cup sugar
⅓ cup water

- Empty cake mix and lemon pudding into a mixing bowl and combine gently.
- Combine all other cake ingredients and pour into dry mixture,

beat at high speed for 3 minutes.
- Pour batter into a greased tube pan and bake at 350° for 45 minutes.
- Just before taking cake from the oven, melt together the sauce ingredients.
- Turn cake out onto a plate with a rim.
- Use a knitting needle to poke holes over top surface of cake.
- Immediately drizzle the melted sauce over the top, a little at a time, allowing it to soak in evenly. (This must be done when the cake is hot or it doesn't soak through.)
- Refrigerate overnight.
- Serve cold with whipped cream.

~~~

Sea Beef, or a Whale of a Cargo

In 1848 the French whaler Captain Morin sailed into Victoria and traded 180 gallons of Sperm Whale oil for 53½ barrels of potatoes and 1,054 pounds of fresh meat. By 1860 Victoria was a base for whaling in the Pacific Northwest, and ships were not only loading vegetables before leaving for the Queen Charlottes, but were also catching Humpback Whales in Saanich Inlet and Georgia Strait.

During the First World War, whale meat was being actively marketed on the west coast at 10 cents per pound. The local press encouraged the use of this "sea beef" by publishing recipes for "Whale Meat Roll," "Whale Meat Shepherd's Pie," and "Whale Stew." However, the marketing met some resistance, as the butchers felt the meat should be carried by fishmongers because it came from the sea.

In these days of declining whale populations, eating whales is certainly not politically correct, though the meat continues to be a delicacy in Japan. Consequently, we do not offer a recipe. However, in salute to the efforts of many agencies to end commercial whaling, we offer Sea Shepherd's Pie.

SEA SHEPHERD'S PIE

Originally made with leftover meat and gravy, but now more popular when made from scratch with fresh ground beef.
Serves 6.

1½ lbs ground beef
1 cup onion, chopped
2 garlic cloves, minced
½ tsp thyme
½ tsp savory
salt and pepper
¼ cup flour
2 cups beef stock
1 tsp Worcestershire sauce
2 medium carrots, peeled and sliced
6 large potatoes
1 cup milk
knob butter
1 egg, lightly beaten
Parmesan cheese, grated

- In a large Dutch oven, brown ground beef, breaking up large pieces.
- Add the garlic and the onions and cook until transparent.
- Drain off excess fat.
- Stir in thyme, savory and salt and pepper to taste.
- Add a little stock to the flour, combine into a paste, then mix in the rest of the stock.
- Add stock mixture to the meat in a steady stream, stirring all the time.
- Add Worcestershire sauce and carrots.
- Simmer partially covered, stirring often, until thick, and the carrots are soft.
- Check and adjust seasoning.
- Spread meat in a 10-cup baking dish, set aside to cool.
- Peel and boil potatoes in salted water until soft.
- Beat egg with a fork.
- Mash potatoes with milk, butter and half of beaten egg, add salt and pepper if desired.
- Spread potatoes carefully over meat. (We find it easiest to spoon on from the outsides in, then smooth across with a fork.)
- Brush with last of egg, sprinkle with grated Parmesan cheese and bake at 400° for 20 minutes or until bubbling and the topping is golden.

Running the Rum

One of the more risky ventures out of Victoria was the rumrunning trade. During the early years of the century, the temperance movement led to the passing of "dry" laws in the various provinces of Canada and the United States. British Columbia went dry during World War I, and was one of the first provinces to abandon prohibition in 1920. Fortunately for Victoria's well-established bootlegging fraternity, U.S. prohibition continued to 1933, when the trade ceased to be profitable.

Although liquor became illegal for the public, it was still made for export purposes. The exception to the rule was that wonderfully elastic phrase "medicinal purposes." It was remarked that during prohibition, there was usually a medical epidemic around Christmastime.

Prohibition was eventually abandoned because it didn't work. Liquor was made illegally in stills, and sold illegally in "blind pigs" even in the most respected of neighbourhoods.

Johnny Schnarr was one of a number of rumrunners who worked out of Victoria in the twenties. He moored at Raymond's Wharf at the end of Belleville Street, loading liquor legally, running it down the coast to the States and unloading it illegally.

This trade was a wonderful stimulant to the local boatbuilding business. As the Coast Guard got more powerful craft, Johnny and his associates had a series of even speedier boats built, often in Victoria. Their sleek craft would set out in the morning and reach the U.S. coast the same evening, so they could unload after dark. Then they would head back to Canada, hopefully arriving the next morning in time for the crew to have breakfast at the Poodle Dog Café.

On less smooth runs, any combination of Coast Guards, cops, customs, hijackers, engine trouble, floating driftwood, fires onboard, storms or fog made the business less appealing. Johnny was perhaps fortunate in that the most direct damage alcohol did to him was when a champagne cork caught him in the eye while celebrating the birth of his son.

FESTIVE RUM PUNCH

Now that we no longer need to be "ill" to imbibe, Christmas can be celebrated in traditional style (at least by non-drivers) with this festive punch.

3 whole cardamom seeds
8 whole cloves
1 cinnamon stick
1 wide strip orange peel
1½ cups water
¼ cup blanched almonds
½ cup light raisins
26-oz bottle Bordeaux or Burgundy
½ bottle Cognac
26-oz bottle rum

- Tie the seeds, cloves, cinnamon and peel in a cheesecloth bag, place in the water in an enamelled pot and bring to boil. Simmer covered for 10 minutes.
- Add almonds and raisins and simmer another 10 minutes.
- Add wine, rum, cognac and bring almost to the boil.
- Remove immediately from heat and store in a cool place overnight to let the flavours develop.
- When ready to serve, remove spice bag and gently reheat but don't boil.
- Serve in warmed mugs or glasses containing a few almonds and raisins.

WARNING: *This smells so good when it's simmering that if the windows are open, the neighbours are likely to drop in for a taste before it ever gets to the cooled stage.*

~~~~~

Globe Circling Excursions

For many decades Victoria was an important port for the trans-Pacific Empress liners, a series of elegant ships designed to carry not just freight, but passengers. The *Empress of India* was in business in 1891, with accommodation for two hundred first- and second-class passengers, and up to another seven hundred in steerage. Its elegant dining saloon was on the upper deck, with large windows and two long tables. She completed her maiden voyage from Liverpool to Victoria in April 1891, and her regular run from Canada to the Orient allowed the company to offer "Around the World Globe Circling Excursions," to be completed by train and Atlantic liner from the Pacific Coast.

Comfort and cuisine were the main ways in which the Empress liners could attract customers. For first-class passengers, dinner on any one of the Empresses was a splendid affair. Evening dress, linen, fine china and silverware were an essential part of the experience. The menu drew on a great variety of sources. "Dining on a Canadian Pacific liner is a rite. Few hotels on earth present a menu so vast, so varied, so elaborately served. Each liner carries some six hundred different items of food; about three hundred tons of the world's delicacies." The *Empress of Japan* in 1930 also carried two chief bakers, two chief butchers, thirty Chinese cooks, nine pantrymen, six steerage cooks, two mess boys, three bakers, two butchers, four assistant butchers and six assistant bakers.

Although the ships are long gone, some of the elegant china from the dining room can still be seen in the B.C. Maritime Museum. And we can still enjoy the food — why not recreate at home some elements of the fine lunch experience of a lost era, described for us in the purple prose of the publicity pamphlets, and even occasionally in authentic recipes?

⌒⌒

Would you Care to Toy with a Little Pâté?

There was "a special chef for hors d'oeuvres . . . it's worth the trip over just to see those gargantuan trays of magnificently landscaped and hand-embroidered canapés, pâté de foie gras, caviar, truffles, lobster, wheeled into lounges and smoking rooms for you to pick and choose from freely."

CHICKEN LIVER PÂTÉ WITH
BRANDIED CURRANTS

Pâté de foie gras is made with goose liver. This recipe uses the cheaper chicken livers, but adds a touch of decadence with the brandy-soaked currants.

½ cup currants
2 tsp brandy
2 lbs chicken livers
1 cup butter
1 onion, finely chopped
2 garlic cloves, finely minced
½ cup whipping cream
1 tsp dried thyme
½ tsp allspice
salt and pepper

- Soak currants in brandy for 1 hour.
- Cut chicken livers in half, removing any membrane and fat.
- Melt ¼ cup of the butter in a frypan, cook onion and garlic until softened and transparent.
- Add livers and cook for approximately 5 minutes, turning often, until golden brown on outside but still a little pink in the centre.
- Place all ingredients, except currants, brandy, salt and pepper, in a food processor and process until smooth.
- Transfer to a bowl and stir in currants and brandy.
- Season to taste.
- Pack into an 8-cup crock. Cover tightly with plastic wrap and refrigerate for at least 3 hours.
- Will keep for up to 4 days.

Eye-Dazzling Salads

"Each noon a truly wonderful cold table appears, attended by high-hatted, white-gloved chefs with gleaming knives. There will be famous Melton Mowbray Pie, the traditional Boar's Head, candied and glazed and frilled with medieval magnificence, tremendous pink jellied fish . . . handsomely decorated cold chicken . . . hams unbelievably savory to the nostrils . . . salads dazzling to the eye and appetite."

GRAPE AND TURKEY SALAD

An *attractive salad that is a meal in itself.*
Serves 8 to 10.

Salad Ingredients
5 cups cooked turkey, chopped
2 cups cantaloupe melon balls
2 cups seedless green grapes
1 cup almonds, slivered
1 cup celery, finely chopped
1 small red onion, cut in fine rings
1 red pepper, diced
1 butter lettuce

Dressing
1 cup plain yogurt
1 cup mayonnaise
1 Tbsp lemon juice
1 tsp curry powder
1 tsp ginger
salt and pepper

- Combine all salad ingredients except lettuce in a bowl.
- In a smaller bowl mix all the dressing ingredients with a whisk.
- Pour dressing over salad ingredients and toss.
- Cover and refrigerate for 2 hours to meld flavours.
- Line a large platter with the butter lettuce. Mound the turkey salad on top.

A DELIGHTFUL CEREMONY

"You never dreamed that eating could be so delightful a ceremony," said the pamphlets, but for special occasions the chefs surpassed themselves. The 1937 Coronation dinner on the Empress of Canada had twelve courses, including *Caviar aux Blinis, Terrine de Foie-Gras Truffée, Tortue verte en Tasse, Mousseline de Saumon Nantua, Sell d'Agneau Roti, Sauce Menthe, Asperges Princess, Soufflé au Chocolat, Sabayon.*

most foolproof rice, Steamed red snapper with fermented black beans

HMS Champion *enters dry dock at Esquimalt, while her sailors, no doubt, paint the town red*

~~~

Continental Confections

The ships served "continental confections that would delight the hearts of epicures," but the dessert recipes that have survived are for more solid fare. The Empresses used this sauce for a steamed ginger pudding. But steamed puddings are a little too stodgy for the modern diet, so we suggest you try this over home-poached or canned pears.

BRANDY SAUCE

Serves 6.

2 Tbsp butter
1/3 cup sugar
1/2 cup boiling water
2 tsp cornstarch
1/2 cup milk
2 egg yolks
2 to 4 Tbsp brandy

- Melt butter in saucepan, add sugar and boiling water.
- Dissolve cornstarch with 2 tablespoons of the milk.
- Beat egg yolks with a fork, then beat in remainder of milk and add the dissolved cornstarch.
- Stir into the saucepan and continue stirring constantly until it thickens — about 10 minutes.
- Remove from heat and stir in brandy.
- Serve hot or cold over steamed pudding (or pears).
- To finish the meal with a decadence and "delightful ceremony" worthy of the Empress line, serve the sauce with the chocolate quiche on page 40, with coffee and a glass of brandy.

VICTORIANS AND FOOD: MIKE LACASSE

Mike is chef on Her Majesty's Canadian Ship Yukon, and is a man with his hands full. The Yukon is a Mackenzie Class Destroyer commissioned in 1963, and still in use as a training ship, so Mike has to keep a crew of nearly two hundred and up to sixty trainees happy at all times. He does this by providing an endless supply of nourishing and tasty meals, round the clock, both in port or at sea.

Mike, originally from Montreal, trained before he enlisted. After nineteen years in the Navy, he is in charge of a staff of eight cooks, and runs a narrow galley complex snaking through the centre of the ship – a space he called compact and we called impossible. The idea of cooking for two hundred in it was mind-boggling; there was certainly no room for anything to go wrong. Occasionally accidental spills occur, usually when the ship heels over in a tight turn when on manoeuvres. Once a huge container of rice was emptied on the galley floor, forming a sticky carpet that the crew slipped and slithered over until it could be cleaned up. Luckily no one was injured.

Mike is also responsible for endless food storage and deep-freeze lockers only accessible down steep companionways. He showed us their entrances and demonstrated how his crew climbs these ladders while carrying enormous supply packages and coping with huge waves. Pretty impressive.

The Navy certainly provides support for its chefs. It has its own training program, then each ship is provided with seven volumes of recipes in two languages, and an endless supply of forms facilitates bulk ordering when in port. But the ingenious chef can use some ideas of his own. Mike regularly adapts recipes from his own books. He also has to know how to obtain fresh vegetables in a strange port, and how to arm-twist travelling service personnel into ordering a treat of fresh lobsters while on leave in Nova Scotia, or carrying deli cheese back from Montreal.

The Yukon's menu is endlessly varied – from hot soup all round when on manoeuvres, to special banquets featuring Canadian delicacies when "showing the flag" for Queen Elizabeth, the King and Queen of Sweden and other dignitaries, to massive cocktail parties when the Yukon makes formal visits to friendly ports.

The chef maintains ship's traditions – the Yukon always serves steak, eggs and champagne for breakfast on the last day at sea. But his main role is that of keeping the crew happy. "Yup," says Mike. "I'm the morale guy on board." He does not balk at serving pizza to everyone on board when they're homesick (even if it means getting up at 3 AM to take the orders), or cooking a hometown favourite, or even rushing around in the mid-afternoon with unannounced ice cream cones to keep spirits up. And how does he relax when he gets home to Esquimalt after slaving over a hot galley? He likes to do the cooking.

~~~

Esquimalt Today

Serious development of Esquimalt started in 1855, when a naval hospital was built in anticipation of battles with the Russians across the Pacific. By 1865, it was an official naval base, and gradually a town grew up close to the base. Actually the town was too close; several buildings, including the church, had to be moved when gun emplacements were built and the base was enlarged. Nowadays the town of Esquimalt has become part of the greater Victoria area, but is still a Navy town, though since 1910 the Navy has been proudly Canadian not British. Thousands of dollars are annually pumped into the Esquimalt and Victoria economies from the base as food supplies, housing, labour and services are in constant demand. Currently there is an open dockyard policy, so any member of the Canadian public can check in for a visit. It's a most picturesque dockyard. Many of the historic red brick buildings from the last century are still there, including the building where the grog was stored (complete with wrought-iron gates to deter break-ins), and the admiral's house, which is gorgeous and must have been a favourite place for elegant receptions. We were lucky enough to get invited aboard a ship, the *Yukon*, for lunch. The facilities were a little cramped, but the food fantastic, so naval hospitality is still legendary.

GREEN JELLYBEAN DAY

One naval tradition has the sailor returning from a long voyage bringing a pocketful of green jellybeans for his children. These are scattered on the lawn while the offspring scramble for as many as possible. The object, of course, is not so much to amuse the kids, as to secure the returning sailor some uninterrupted time with his wife. The time can be prolonged by telling the kids there are one hundred beans when in fact there are only ninety-nine. Thanks to this custom, the day the sailor returns is known as "Green Jellybean Day."

IRISH TEA BRACK

Many recipes in the early naval tradition included alcohol. This tea bread also utilized leftover tea.
Makes 3 loaves.

3 cups sultanas (light-coloured raisins)
3 cups raisins (dark-coloured raisins)
2½ cups brown sugar
1½ cups cold tea
1½ cups Irish whiskey
4 cups flour
3 tsp baking powder
1 tsp ground ginger
1 tsp allspice
1 tsp cinnamon
3 eggs
liquid honey

- Mix fruit and sugar in a bowl, add the tea and whiskey, stir, cover with plastic and let soak overnight.
- Sift together the dry ingredients.
- Beat the eggs, add to the fruit mixture alternately with the flour mixture. Combine well.
- Grease and flour three loaf pans (8 x 4 x 3 inches).
- Divide batter between pans, bake at 300° for approximately 1½ hours.
- Remove pans from the oven, let cool for 10 minutes, then turn out loaves.
- Brush tops with liquid honey to give a fine glaze.

VEGETABLE BEEF SOUP

Naval food menus move with the times, and currently include such dishes as Goulash, Sauerbraten, Tourtière, Jambalaya and African Lamb Stew, as well as vegetarian dishes. But essentially the Navy remains a "meat and potatoes" outfit. For a taste of older style rib-sticking food, try this soup. Unfortunately, the recipe didn't specify the size of pot needed to cook it in.
Serves 100 with one cup each. Double if you wish to serve the entire ship's crew.

20 lbs beef bones
5¼ gallons water
pepper
ground cloves
2½ qts celery, diced
¾ qts onions, sliced
1¼ qts turnips, diced
1¼ qts carrots, diced
2 qts potatoes, diced
13 lbs canned tomatoes
4 ozs salt
2 ozs Worcestershire sauce
¼ lb egg noodles
2 garlic cloves (really!)

- Saw bones into pieces, cook separately for 2 hours.
- Remove meat from bones and put meat back into stock.
- Cover and heat to boiling point.
- Add pepper, cloves, onions, celery, turnips, tomatoes, carrots, garlic and salt. Mix well.
- Cover and heat to boiling, simmer for 40 minutes.
- Add potatoes, simmer 10 minutes.
- Add noodles, simmer 10 minutes.
- Add Worcestershire sauce and serve.

9

Chinatown – Where the East meets the West

Step into the Far East. Turn from Government Street onto Fisgard and walk under the Gate of Harmonious Interest into Canada's oldest Chinatown. The stores, spilling exuberantly over the sidewalk, are a wonderful visual and olfactory feast. Shopping here is an adventure. Somehow the fruits and vegetables seem brighter, fresher and have an air of intrigue missing from the supermarket. The pile of familiar green peppers nestle against a giant winter melon split with a lethal-looking cleaver, ready for you to serve yourself. A basket full of lemon grass flanks a variety of mushrooms, only one of which you recognize, and the lettuce mounds around a waist-high ceramic pot containing thousand-year-old eggs.

Don't be deterred by hearing only Chinese spoken; most of the residents speak English if you need to ask a question. And don't be awed by the unusual variety of produce. Wade in, buy whatever you fancy, then ask a few questions. We've been given recipes at the checkout, and graphic preparation methods in mime on the sidewalk. All it takes is a smile, genuine interest and a willingness to try anything.

As you walk along, the nose quivers and the taste buds drool from the tantalizing hints of herbs and spices flowing from the restaurants. They are varied, and specialize in a variety of Chinese cuisine, from well-known Cantonese favourites to mouth-watering spicy northern cuisine such as Szechuan delicacies like hot and sour soup. If you are looking for cheap but nourishing food, in Chinatown you can still eat a filling bowl of noodle soup with fish balls, accompanied by a hot fresh barbecued pork bun, and have change from $6.

For a different kind of meal, linger over a dim sum lunch, teasing the palate by choosing selections of tiny stuffed dumplings or savoury morsels pushed temptingly by on wagons. Don't worry about identification; the helpings are tastes only, so if one doesn't please your palate, the next one will. Go with friends and share the adventure, but be sure to leave a little space to finish with either an egg custard tart or an almond bun.

Chinese meals are traditionally social occasions and families with children are welcome in most of the restaurants. Children are intrigued by the challenge of chopsticks, and any passing restaurant personnel will be happy to give a chopstick lesson to the uninitiated of any age.

For a special evening out, gather some friends and splash out with a many-course Chinese dinner elegantly served on tablecloths with fresh flowers and candlelight. Chinatown offers styles and selections to suit any pocketbook.

Don't overlook Fan Tan Alley. Once the most notorious part of Victoria, this narrow alley (barely more than one person wide) runs between Fisgard and Pandora streets, and houses interesting shops, boutiques and galleries. Want a set of rice bowls and chopsticks, or a handmade leather belt? How about a Guatemalan jacket? You might find it in Fan Tan Alley. One Chinese gift store is a must-see. It starts on Fisgard and wanders along beside Fan Tan Alley through a variety of small and increasingly warren-like rooms. In one of the last rooms is a little cell. This is all that remains of a notorious gambling saloon at the turn of the century. The cell – literally a hole in the wall – housed the cashier safely behind bars. The original abacus and tokens are on display with a variety of other artifacts.

Feeling adventurous? Take your basket, purchase your ingredients on Fisgard Street and try these recipes at home.

FAME AT LAST?

Victoria's Chinatown was the set for part of the 1989 Goldie Hawn and Mel Gibson movie Bird on a Wire. *Although a mediocre movie, it's worth seeing for the great chase scene – on a motorbike – through Fan Tan Alley. Parts of more than fourteen feature films have been made in Victoria in recent years.*

~~~

Dinner — Chinese Style

Here are some simple dishes for a Chinese dinner. All the ingredients can be found in Victoria's Chinatown. Shop the morning of the dinner so everything is at its peak of freshness. We take guests along for the experience and put them in charge of choosing ingredients and later preparing one of the recipes. This cuts down the preparation work for a Chinese dinner and most guests love to be involved.

Be aware while planning the dinner that the dishes should be a feast for the eye as well as the taste buds. Use your prettiest platters to serve. Balance — or the yin/yang principle — affects the choice of dishes. A smooth and subtle dish should be balanced by one with a crunchy texture, a spicy dish by a sweet one, etc. As a Chinese dinner consists of many dishes, you do not need to double the recipes, just increase the number of dishes. The rule of thumb is one dish per person, plus a rice or noodle dish. They are served together in the centre of the table and the guests mix and match tastes. The serving amounts given are based on being part of a many-course dinner.

EASY WINTER MELON SOUP

Purchasing winter melon for this easy recipe is a good first introduction to a Chinatown grocery. The winter melons look similar to watermelons, but are a paler green. Buy only what you need. A cleaver will be found beside it. Cut yourself a healthy slice and take it over to the cashier. They will weigh it and calculate the price. Buy the dried Chinese mushrooms at the same store. They are usually packaged in a plastic bag, but sometimes are found loose.
    Makes 4 one-cup servings.

1 lb winter melon
6 dried Chinese mushrooms
1 - ⅛ inch-thick slice of precooked ham
3 cups skimmed chicken stock, fresh or canned
1 green onion, finely chopped

- Place the dried mushrooms in a small bowl, cover with ½ cup of warm water and leave to soak for 30 minutes. Drain. Cut away the tough stems and discard. Slice the caps.
- Prepare the winter melon. Scrape away the inner seeds and stringy fibre, peel and cut into 1 inch pieces.

- Remove any fat from ham and chop into thin strips 2 inches long.
- Check stock for seasoning and adjust to taste.
- Finely chop the green onion.
- In a large saucepan combine the chicken stock, melon and mushrooms and bring to the boil. Reduce immediately to simmer, cover and cook for 15 minutes.
- Ladle into individual bowls or a large tureen. Stir in the chopped ham and sprinkle the finely chopped green onion on top.

TEA LEAF EGGS

Many westerners find the concept of thousand-year-old eggs difficult, so here is an alternative hors d'oeuvre recipe for eggs that can be done the night before the dinner party. Cut the finished eggs in wedges and serve as a finger food at the beginning of the meal. We serve them after the soup. They are a good conversation promoter while we are in the kitchen stir-frying the next dishes.
Serves 6 to 8.

6 eggs
4 cups cold water
1 Tbsp salt
1 whole star anise or 8 sections
2 Tbsp soy sauce
2 tea bags

- Place the eggs in a saucepan and cover with 2 cups of the cold water. Simmer them gently for 20 minutes. Leave them in the water to cool. Drain when cool enough to handle.
- Tap the eggs gently all over with the back of a teaspoon (or roll gently on the counter) until the shells are covered with a network of fine cracks. (Be gentle; pieces of shell should not drop off.)
- Place the 2 remaining cups of cold water in the saucepan along with the salt, anise, soya sauce and tea bags. Stir, and add the eggs.
- Bring quickly to the boil, then reduce heat to a low simmer. Cover pan and simmer for 2 hours, adding extra boiling water as needed to keep the eggs covered.
- Turn off the heat and leave eggs cooling in the water at room temperature for 8 hours or overnight.
- Just before serving, carefully remove the shells. The whites should be marbled with thin dark lines.
- Cut into wedges and serve cold from a platter lined with lettuce.

THE LEGENDARY THOUSAND-YEAR-OLD EGG

Relax, they are not really a thousand years old, only a few months! These are duck eggs coated with a paste of ashes, lime and salt and buried in clay for several months. They are sold individually. Scraped and de-shelled, they have rich translucent hues of blue and green, the most vivid green being the yolk. The texture is creamy like avocado flesh, and they are so rich that only a taste per person is needed. They are often served cold at the beginning of a meal.

If the eggs don't tempt you, the large ceramic pots they are shipped in might. These are sold when emptied and make attractive patio planters.

Rice, Everyone?

Rice, the eastern staple, is now enormously popular on the west coast. In the old days, however, the Chinese servants were not allowed to cook Chinese-style for many of their employers. If your family eats a lot of it, treat yourself to one of the electric rice cookers found by the dozen in every store in Chinatown. There is a wonderful variety of rice available. If you'd like a change from white or brown rice, try jasmine-scented or basmati rice.

ALMOST FOOLPROOF RICE

White rice doubles in volume when cooked, so adjust the formula below for the number of guests you are feeding.
Makes 4 half-cup servings.

1 cup long grain white rice
2 cups water

- Rinse the rice well in cold water, drain.
- Place rice and water in a large saucepan. Bring quickly to the boil over high heat. Boil for 2 or 3 minutes until small craters appear in the surface of the rice.
- Cover the pan tightly, reduce heat to low and cook for 20 minutes (don't peek).
- Turn off the heat but do not uncover the pan. Let rest for 10 minutes.
- Remove lid, fluff with a fork or chopsticks and serve.

EGGPLANT AND DRIED SHRIMP

The familiar eggplant can be used, but the small Chinese eggplants are delicious and save time, as they don't need peeling. Approximately two to three inches in length and one inch wide with the same purple skin, they are succulent, tender and sweeter than their larger sister. The tiny dried shrimps come in plastic packages, often found inside the stores in the same area as dried mushrooms.
Serves 4 to 6.

½ cup small dried shrimp
1 cup hot water
1 lb eggplant
8 garlic cloves, peeled
4 Tbsp peanut or vegetable oil
1 Tbsp soy sauce
1 Tbsp Chinese rice wine or pale dry sherry
1 tsp sugar

- In a small bowl, cover the dried shrimp with hot water and soak for 30 minutes. Drain off the water and save.
- Wash eggplant. If using the large ones, peel and cut into strips approximately 2 inches long and ½ inch wide. Top and tail small Chinese ones and split in half lengthways.
- Using a garlic press, crush each garlic clove.
- Combine soy sauce, wine and sugar.
- Preheat a wok or frying pan for 30 seconds. Pour in the oil and swirl around for another 30 seconds.
- Add eggplant and garlic, turn heat to low and fry, stirring and turning gently until lightly brown, approximately 10 to 15 minutes.
- Add soy sauce mixture, shrimp and ⅓ cup of shrimp water.
- Cover pan and simmer over low heat for 10 minutes or until the liquid is absorbed.
- Spoon onto a platter. This dish can be served hot immediately or prepared ahead and served cold.

STIR-FRIED SNOW PEAS WITH
CHINESE VEGETABLES

Buy fresh snow or sugar peas for this dish. The tender edible pods add a lovely crunchy texture to a Chinese meal. Do not overcook. For ease of preparation use canned bamboo shoots.
Serves 4 to 6.

1 lb snow or sugar peas
½ cup canned whole bamboo shoots
6 dried Chinese mushrooms
½ cup warm water
1 tsp salt, or less, to taste
½ tsp sugar
1 garlic clove, chopped
2 Tbsp peanut or vegetable oil

- In a small bowl, cover the dried mushrooms with warm water and soak for 30 minutes. Drain, reserving 2 tablespoons of the liquid. Cut away and discard the tough mushroom stems. Cut each cap into quarters.
- Top and tail snow peas, removing any strings.
- Drain, rinse and pat dry bamboo shoots. Slice into ⅛ inch-thick triangles.
- Preheat wok for 30 seconds. Swirl oil around and preheat for a further 30 seconds.
- Turn heat to medium (do not allow oil to smoke).
- Drop in chopped garlic and stir-fry 10 seconds.
- Toss in the bamboo shoots and mushrooms, stir-fry for 2 minutes.
- Add snow peas, sugar, salt and the 2 tablespoons reserved mushroom water. Stir-fry on high for approximately 1½ minutes until water has evaporated.
- Transfer to a platter and serve.

Getting Steamed Up

Steaming is a simple and nutritious way to cook fish. If you don't possess a steamer, buy one of the cheap traditional bamboo ones from Chinatown. They come in a variety of sizes, so choose the one that will sit comfortably on your largest pot. Don't forget to pick up the accompanying lid, usually sold separately. The steamers are decorative and effective and once you possess one you will find other uses for it. (We have several that we use to carry elegant picnic platters out to the beach, and our daughter uses them in the galley of a sailboat, as they are light and allow her to cook a couple of dishes over the same burner.)

BLOOD, SWEAT AND TIES

The Chinese labourers literally helped to build Canada. Hundreds of thousands sweated over the railroad swinging pickaxes, laying ties and track and pounding spikes, for without the rail connection B.C. refused to join confederation. It is said that for every mile of track laid a Chinese labourer was buried, yet there are no Chinese present in the famous photo taken at the driving of the last spike.

STEAMED RED SNAPPER
WITH FERMENTED BLACK BEANS

This recipe can be steaming over a back ring while you are stir-frying another at the front. The fermented black beans are usually sold in plastic bags. Unused beans should be stored in tightly covered containers in the fridge. They will keep for over six months. If they dry out add a little oil.
Serves 4 to 6.

1½ lbs red snapper fillets
2 Tbsp fermented black beans
1 Tbsp soy sauce
1 Tbsp Chinese rice wine or dry sherry
½ tsp sugar
1 Tbsp peanut or vegetable oil
½ tsp salt
1 Tbsp grated ginger root
2 green onions, cut into 2 inch lengths, including the tops

- Wash fish fillets and pat dry.
- Arrange fillets on a heatproof plate that fits inside the steamer; leave ½ inch space around the edge for steam to rise. Sprinkle with salt.
- Coarsely chop the black beans. Place in a bowl with the soy sauce, oil, wine and sugar and stir well to make a sauce.
- Drizzle the sauce over the fillets, sprinkle the grated ginger on top, then lay the green onions across in a nice design.
- Have enough boiling water in the bottom pot to come within 1½ inches of the steamer. Place the plate in the steamer, cover and place the steamer over the boiling pot.
- Steam the fish for about 10 to 15 minutes or until firm to the touch. (Keep the water at a continuous boil and add to it if necessary.)
- Lift out plate, place on top of another, and serve.

FROM HORRORS TO HONOURS

In the early years, Chinese immigrants were considered aliens and subjected to indignities such as the head tax, and employed only as servants. Fortunately, times have changed. The Chinese community is an important and respected part of the fabric of Victoria, and its contributions to the city are manyfold. Victorians celebrated in 1988 when David Lam, a respected Chinese businessman from Vancouver, became B.C.'s lieutenant governor, the Queen's representative, and moved into Government House on Rockland Avenue.

SWEET AND SOUR PORK

Sweet and sour dishes are some of the best known of the Chinese cuisine. This recipe is ideal for a dinner, as you can fry the meat a little ahead of time and keep it warm in the oven. Assemble the sauce ingredients ahead of time. Cook sauce and combine with meat at the last minute.
Serves 6.

Pork Preparation

1 lb lean, boneless pork
1 egg, lightly beaten
1/4 cup flour
1/4 cup cornstarch
1/2 tsp salt
1/4 cup chicken stock
3 cups peanut or vegetable oil

- Trim any fat off the pork and cut into 1 inch cubes.
- In a large bowl combine all other ingredients except the oil, toss in the pork and stir until well coated.
- Preheat oven to 250°.
- Pour 3 cups of oil into wok and heat until just before smoking. Quickly add half the pork cubes, one at a time, and fry for 5 to 6 minutes until a crisp golden brown. (Regulate the heat so the pork does not burn.) Remove meat with a slotted spoon and keep warm in the oven. Repeat process with the second half of the pork.
- Discard the cooking oil and wipe wok with paper towel.

Sweet and Sour Sauce

1 Tbsp peanut or vegetable oil
1 tsp garlic, chopped
1 large green pepper
1 medium carrot
½ cup chicken stock
4 Tbsp sugar
4 Tbsp red wine vinegar
1 tsp soy sauce
1 Tbsp cornstarch
2 Tbsp cold water

- De-seed the green pepper and cut into 1 inch squares.
- Peel and slice carrot, ¼ inch thick pieces.
- Heat wok for 30 seconds. Swirl tablespoon of oil around for another 30 seconds, turn down heat and add garlic, green pepper and carrot. Stir-fry for approximately 2 minutes until they slightly change colour (don't let them burn).
- Add chicken stock, sugar, vinegar and soy sauce and boil, stirring until sugar is dissolved.
- Combine cornstarch and water and add to the wok. Cook a little longer, stirring constantly until thick and clear.
- Pour over the precooked pork and serve immediately.

THE GATE OF HARMONIOUS INTEREST

A recent and spectacular addition to Chinatown is Tong Ji Men, the Gate of Harmonious Interest, dedicated in 1981. The gate is an obvious meeting place and has become one of Victoria's most photographed landmarks. It was designed in the city, and constructed here with materials from Taiwan. Decorations include dragons, phoenixes, lions and plum blossoms. Half the cost was provided by donations from the Chinese and non-Chinese communities, and the other half by the province. The stone lions were gifts from the city of Suzhou, Victoria's sister city in China.

CHICKEN WITH CASHEWS
AND HOISIN SAUCE

Hoisin sauce is a sweetish, reddish brown sauce made from soya beans mixed with spices including garlic and chili. It's sold in bottles in Chinatown and will keep for months. Despite the hint of chilies in the sauce, this dish is quite mild. If you'd like to spice it up, at the last moment stir in a small amount of red chili and garlic paste, also found in jars in the stores.
Serves 6.

2 whole chicken breasts, boneless and skinned
1 Tbsp cornstarch
1 Tbsp Chinese rice wine or dry sherry
1 Tbsp soy sauce
1/4 cup peanut or vegetable oil
2 garlic cloves, chopped
1 green pepper
6 water chestnuts, canned
6 fresh mushrooms
2 Tbsp hoisin sauce
1/4 to 1/2 tsp red chili and garlic paste (optional)
1/2 cup roasted cashews

- De-seed the pepper and cut in 1 inch squares.
- Slice the water chestnuts and mushrooms.
- Cut the chicken breasts into 1/2 inch squares, place in a well-made plastic bag (check that there are no holes). Add the cornstarch and, holding the neck of the bag firmly, shake until the chicken is coated.
- Open the bag, pour in the wine and soy sauce. Shake again to coat.
- Preheat wok 30 seconds. Pour in half the oil and swirl around, then turn heat to moderate.
- Add half chopped garlic and stir-fry for 10 seconds.
- Add mushroom and green pepper and stir-fry for 2 to 3 minutes.
- Scoop out the vegetables and reserve on a heated platter.
- Add remaining oil, heat to almost smoking, swirl, add remaining garlic, stir-fry 5 seconds.
- Drop in chicken; stir-fry briskly for 2 to 3 minutes, until white and firm.
- Add hoisin sauce and stir well.
- Add the reserved vegetables and cook for 1 minute longer. At this point, if desired, stir in the chili and garlic sauce.
- Transfer the entire contents to a heated serving platter, sprinkle with cashew nuts and serve.

...mpkin soup, Asparagus with mustard cream sauce, Herbed red potato salad

Around 1914, you could have bought fish on the street from this Chinese salesman

~~~

Finishing Touch

Dessert is not usually served at a Chinese dinner, but a large dish of orange wedges garnished with mint leaves makes an attractive and simple ending to the meal. It also cleanses the palate. If you would like to share the fun of fortune cookies with your guests, they can be purchased in bulk in some of the Chinatown groceries and passed around at this point. Our favourite fortune cookie? The one that told Andrea: "You have a way with words; utilize it."

FOR ALL THE TEA IN CHINA

Green tea is traditionally drunk throughout a meal. In many restaurants a pot of tea is automatically placed on the table as soon as you are seated. When your teapot is emptied, upending the lid on top of the pot will signal the staff, and the pot will be whisked away and refilled with a fresh brew of tea. You can do this as many times as you wish.

10

Ethnic Flavours

Victoria's British facade has been promoted for years by the Chamber of Commerce but, in reality, it is only one aspect of the city. Victoria has always been an exciting and vibrant mix of many cultures who add their own stamp and pizazz to the so-called British roots. The cultural groups currently residing in Victoria are too numerous to list, but several are represented by delightful ethnic restaurants or specialty food outlets, or even unusual buildings in different areas of the city.

In fact, the British were always given a run for their money. The First Nations were here for centuries, and the Spanish explorers arrived before the British. Scarcely was the colony established when the influx of miners brought many nationalites whose first language was not English. The tent city was enlivened by arguments and discussions where German, French, Norwegian, Russian and Italian voices intermingled with Irish, Welsh and Scottish accents. The resulting differences were sometimes buried over a shared campfire, a drink and the joint raising of voices in snatches of ethnic songs, and other times resulted in fights to the death.

By the 1860s there was a large black population, many of them freed slaves, encouraged to settle in Victoria by James Douglas, who was himself a quarter black. Humboldt Street was once known as Kanaka Row, because of the number of Hawaiian sailors who lived there. There was the Songhees Native village, Chinatown and contingents of Italians and Greeks working in the fishing fleet centred in Victoria. They had also arrived with the miners and decided to stay.

By 1891 Victoria boasted a German Lutheran church where people worshipped in the German language, and a synagogue. Add all this to the British establishment, and the view of Victoria becomes much more than a British ghetto — and a whole lot more exciting.

Once a year a multicultural folkfest is held in Centennial Square (the park by City Hall), to celebrate Victoria's cultural mix. Ethnic food tempts the taste buds, unusual music pleases the ear and colourful costumes dazzle the eye. This taste of multicultural Victoria is barely enough to whet the appetite, so here's a selection of tasty ethnic and celebratory recipes that reflect Victoria's more exotic side. We've included a few suggestions as to where you can purchase the ingredients. Just visiting the specialty shops will give you a whole new slant on Victoria.

Our Home and Native Land

The First Peoples Festival held in Victoria in mid-summer celebrates the songs, stories and dances of the West Coast's aboriginal people, and showcases the art stemming from their many traditions. There's drumming and chanting, totem carving, displays and performances, food and a chance to meet and talk with some Native artists. This is the living culture as opposed to a museum exhibit, reflecting current situations and concerns, and shouldn't be missed by anyone interested in the current role of Canada's First Peoples.

WILD RASPBERRIES AND HONEY

Desserts are not a big item in First Nations cuisine, but almost every group knows the tradition of mixing crushed wild fruits with honey. This is something that is shared by other cultures, who refer to the resulting syrup as "coulis" and pour it over chocolate cake or chocolate pâté.

Serves 6.

1 qt wild raspberries or blackberries
2 cups liquid honey

- Crush the raspberries in the liquid honey with a potato masher.
- Serve in small bowls.

꿈

A Black Mark on our Past

By the middle of the 1860s there was a community of several hundred blacks in Victoria, many of them freed slaves from tobacco plantations in the southern United States. At least one black family came to Victoria from Louisiana, where Creole cooking was created. Records show that they were poor and regularly could only afford to eat "a mess of greens" — a sort of stir-fry of garden vegetables, with lots of cabbage and turnip. But Creole cooking at its best featured oysters, shrimp, snapper and a pungent tomato sauce flavoured with chilies and garlic, and one would like to think that occasionally the families enjoyed Victoria's seafood. Despite sympathetic support from James Douglas, this early black community was not welcomed in Victoria. Apart from some settlement on nearby Salt Spring Island, they dispersed to other parts of Canada or gradually filtered back to the States. We offer a classic Creole dish, in their memory.

CREOLE SHRIMP

Serves 6.

12 firm ripe tomatoes
   or 4 cups canned tomatoes, drained
3 lbs medium shrimp, uncooked (20 to 24 to the lb)
½ cup vegetable oil
2 cups onion, chopped
1 cup green pepper, chopped
1 cup celery, chopped
2 tsp garlic, minced
1 cup water
2 bay leaves
1 Tbsp paprika
½ tsp cayenne pepper
1 tsp salt
2 Tbsp cornstarch, mixed with ¼ cup water
6 cups long grain rice, freshly boiled

- Skin fresh tomatoes or thoroughly drain canned tomatoes, and coarsely chop.
- Shell and devein shrimp. Wash under running water and dry thoroughly.
- Heat oil in a heavy 4-quart Dutch oven until a light haze forms. Add onions, green pepper, celery and garlic and keep stirring until vegetables are soft and onions translucent. Do not brown.
- Stir in tomatoes, 1 cup of water, bay leaves, paprika, cayenne and salt, and bring to the boil over high heat.
- Reduce heat to low, partially cover pot and simmer, stirring occasionally, for 20 to 25 minutes or until it is thick enough to hold its shape almost solidly on a spoon.
- Stir in the shrimp and continue to simmer for approximately 5 minutes, until shrimp are firm and pink.
- Combine the cornstarch and ¼ cup water and stir well. Add in a steady stream to the shrimp mixture, stirring all the time on low heat until mixture thickens.
- Pick out and discard bay leaves, and check and adjust seasoning.
- Pick out your biggest salad bowl or giant platter. Heap the freshly cooked rice in the middle and ladle the shrimp Creole around it.

Soul Food

Currently a variety of black cultures are represented in Victoria, from Kenya, the United States, South Africa and the West Indies, to name just a few. One day when walking through Market Square courtyard we came upon a reggae concert. We joined in, dancing and swaying to the music, and suddenly became aware that for once we were the obvious minority. We were welcomed and included. By the end of the afternoon Andrea's hair was braided and beaded, and we were satiated with soul music and soul food and a feeling of exuberant exotica we had never expected to find in Victoria. Watch out for the next one; it's really worth attending.

SAUSAGE AND EGGPLANT JAMBALAYA

Serves 4.

½ lb breakfast sausage
½ lb pepperoni sausage
½ cup onion, chopped
¼ cup green pepper, chopped
¼ cup celery, chopped
1 tsp garlic, minced
1¼ cups rice, uncooked
2½ to 3 cups water
½ tsp cayenne pepper
1 tsp salt
2 eggplant, approximately 1 lb each

- Slice both kinds of sausage into ¼ inch slices.
- Fry gently in a heavy pan until they have rendered all their fat. Remove from pan with a slotted spoon and drain on paper towel. Set aside.
- Pour all but 4 tablespoons of fat from skillet. Add onion, green pepper, celery and garlic. Cook gently and stir frequently until vegetables are soft but not brown.
- Add the rice and stir until coated. Add 2½ cups of water, cayenne and salt. Bring to a boil over high heat.
- Peel and stem eggplant and cut into ½ inch cubes.
- Stir sausages and eggplant into boiling rice mixture. Reduce heat to low, cover and simmer for 45 minutes or until eggplant is tender. Check occasionally and add extra water a few tablespoons at a time to prevent burning.
- The jambalaya is cooked when most of the liquid is absorbed by the rice and it's somewhat sticky.
- Check for seasoning and serve at once directly from pot.

⌒

Dancing with Dragons

In the early years the influx of Chinese immigrants did not sit well with Victorians, except for the fact they were considered wonderful servants and most households could afford at least one to do the laundry, cooking and working in the vegetable garden (Emily Carr's family had one called Bong). Plans for early houses automatically designated the servants' quarters as "Chinaman." But most were only allowed to cook English-style for their employers.

Now Chinese food is an everyday option, with Chinese restaurants spotted all over Victoria. If you want to share a very special Chinese celebration, however, attend the Chinese New Year Festivities and watch the dragon dance wind its sinuous way through Chinatown, accompanied by drummers and masked attendants who encourage its every step. There are firecrackers and special banquets to mark this event, and it's a spectacle you'll never forget.

CHICKEN WINGS CHINESE STYLE

12 chicken wings
2 Tbsp soy sauce
2 green onions, chopped
2 tsp ginger root, grated
2 tsp rice wine or dry sherry
2 cups oil
2 Tbsp oyster sauce
1 Tbsp sugar
1 cup water
1 tsp parsley, chopped
sesame oil
sesame seeds

- Wash and dry chicken wings, and place in a medium bowl.
- Pour soy sauce, green onion, grated ginger and wine over wings. Let marinate for 30 minutes. Turn a couple of times.
- Heat oil in wok.
- Add chicken wings 3 at a time and cook until golden. Drain well on paper towel.
- Place oyster sauce, sugar and water in a saucepan . Bring to the boil.
- Add chicken wings, reduce heat and simmer for 15 minutes or until sauce thickens.
- Serve on heated platter, sprinkled with parsley, a few drops of sesame oil and sesame seeds.

~~~

Kanaka Row

I thought I heard the old Man say,
John Kanaka-naka tooriay,
We'll work tomorrow but not today,
John Kanaka-naka tooriay,
Tooriay, oh tooriay,
John Kanaka-naka tooriay
— OLD SEA SHANTY

Kanaka Row was a shanty town that, along with Pendray's Soapworks, ran up the side of James Bay, along what is now Humboldt Street. Kanaka was the commonly used slang term for the Hawaiian sailors who worked on the tall ships beating up the west coast and across the Pacific to Victoria and Vancouver. Dr. Helmcken, son-in-law to James Douglas, records in his journal that, at one time, Fort Victoria had both a Hawaiian steward and cook. The cook was obviously skilful, producing quite a feast on the night recorded. "On comes the soup, then the salmon, then the meats, venison on this occasion and ducks — then the pies." We don't know what pies were served for dessert, probably ones featuring apples or maybe local blackberries. However here is a true taste of Hawaii — a pie featuring fresh pineapple.

PINEAPPLE TART

½ recipe Never-fail Pastry *(see page 48)*
4 cups fresh crushed pineapple
1½ cups sugar

- Make up pastry, roll out, fit into a pie plate and trim. Make the rest into lattice strips for pie top.
- Combine the crushed pineapple and sugar in a heavy saucepan and bring to the boil. Stir often. Let boil uncovered for about 20 minutes, until most of the liquid has evaporated, but do not allow to burn. Cool.
- Spoon pineapple into pastry base. Cover decoratively with lattice strips, sealing and fluting the edges.
- Bake at 375° for approximately 40 minutes or until pastry is golden.

The City of Chimes

Several times throughout the day, Victoria's downtown users are enchanted with the carillon, whose notes soar above the city buildings. The carillon tower, seen at the corner of the museum complex, was donated by British Columbia's Dutch settlers, most of whom came here after the Second World War. In 1970 many Dutch immigrants took part in a nationwide "Thank You Canada Project" to mark the 25th anniversary of the liberation of the Netherlands by the Canadian Army. Those in B.C. donated a carillon as part of Victoria's museum complex. When the carillon's noontime concert reminds you it's time for lunch, head over to the incredible Dutch Bakery on Fort Street. There is almost always a lineup, which is good because the selection is so great you need time to plan what you're going to eat.

DUTCH SPEKULAAS COOKIES

These are traditionally made at Christmas. The dough is pressed into wooden spekulaas boards to make elaborate figures and shapes. Some spekulaas boards can be seen on the walls of the Dutch Bakery. Our Dutch neighbours once lent us a twelve-inch-high antique spekulaas board of St. Nicholas, and Andrea made a cookie each for all the children for St. Nicholas Day on December 6. Usually, though, we just use cookie cutters of gingerbread men, angels, sleighs, etc., and poke a hole in the top of each cookie. When they are baked, we thread a ribbon through and decorate our Christmas tree with them. Any child visiting our house chooses one to take home.

Makes 2 dozen cookies.

2 cups flour
1 cup sugar
½ tsp baking powder
1 tsp cinnamon
½ tsp nutmeg
½ tsp allspice
pinch salt
1 cup butter
1¼ Tbsp milk

- Sift together all the dry ingredients.
- Rub in the butter.
- Add the milk and combine gently with your hand to make a ball of dough.
- Roll out on a floured board until half thick.
- Press into a spekulaas board or cut out shapes with a cookie cutter.
- Bake on ungreased cookie sheets at 350° for 20 minutes or until brown.
- Remove gently. They are fragile when hot, but more robust when cooled.

~~~

From Marble to Munchies

The first Italian of note in Victoria was Carlo Bossi, a marble cutter who came up as miner in 1858, found work in a general store and stayed, eventually opening his own store. He died a wealthy and distinguished citizen. There have been many Italians following in his footsteps, several of whom turned their skills at marble cutting to granite carving; their work adorns many of the older houses and mansions in Victoria. Italian pasta has become a routine modern favourite served in a variety of restaurants, so for a different taste of Italy visit the Italian Bakery on Quadra for traditional breads and cakes. We defy you to walk out without snacking on a strip of tarragon-flavoured focaccia bread. This is also the place to visit just before Easter, when they sell large ornate Italian chocolate Easter eggs. You have to order them early, though, as they sell out fast.

POLLO ALLA DIAVOLA
(BROILED DEVILLED CHICKEN)

Large flat-leafed Italian parsley can be found fresh in many supermarkets. It is sometimes called cilantro or coriander.
Serves 4.

1 cup butter
2 Tbsp olive oil
½ tsp dried chili peppers, crushed
¼ cup onion, finely chopped
2 Tbsp Italian parsley, finely chopped
1 tsp garlic, finely chopped

1 chicken, approximately 2 to 3 lbs, quartered
1 tsp salt
1 lemon, quartered

- Preheat the broiler.
- Melt butter and combine in a small bowl with oil and crushed chilies.
- In another bowl mix together the chopped onion, parsley and garlic. Add 4 teaspoons of the butter-oil mixture and stir to make a paste. Set aside.
- Wash the chicken and pat dry. Brush all surfaces with the butter-oil mixture and lightly salt.
- Arrange skin side down on the broiler rack. Broil 4 inches from the grill for 5 minutes.
- Baste with remaining butter-oil mixture and broil for a further 5 minutes.
- Baste again and turn skin side up. Broil and baste at 5-minute intervals (use pan dripping when you run out of the butter and oil) for another 10 to 15 minutes or until juices run clear when a thigh is pricked.
- With a small metal spatula spread the onion and parsley paste on top of each quarter of chicken, patting it firmly in place.
- Broil for 3 or 4 minutes or until coating is lightly browned.
- Serve on a heated platter, garnish with the lemon quarters and baste with the last of the pan dripping if desired.

~

Stille Nacht And Noisy Nights

Dr. John Sebastian Helmcken was a German who came to Fort Victoria as the fort's medical officer. He died one of the most respected men in the city of Victoria. His house still stands next to the Royal British Columbia Museum, and is a historic site noted for its delightful Christmas program. Helmcken was the forerunner of many German immigrants who helped Victoria grow into a city. Among them are Joseph Lowen, who founded a distillery and a flour business, and Louis Erb, who established the Phoenix Brewing Company. The First World War was an unmitigated disaster for the German families who had settled here. One night, after the sinking of the *Lusitania*, a riot swept through Victoria, wrecking the Blanshard Hotel (formerly the Kaiserhof and run by H. Kostenblader, who was a naturalized British subject) and any other businesses whose proprietors had German-sounding names. Then came the Depression, then the next war. German songs were banned, German foods were no longer served and German accents were definitely suspicious. Thank goodness times change. Imagine life without bratwurst sausage, German beer or "Stille Nacht" — the strains of which can be heard issuing from Helmcken House at Christmastime.

GERMAN RED CABBAGE

Serves 6 to 8.

2 lbs red cabbage
2 Tbsp butter
1 Tbsp sugar
1 onion, grated
2 apples, peeled, cored and diced
4 Tbsp vinegar
salt, to taste
1½ cups water
3 bay leaves
1 onion, studded with 4 whole cloves
¾ cup red wine

- Wash cabbage, core and coarsely grate.
- Melt butter, add sugar and heat gently until brown.
- Add grated onion and diced apple and sauté until brown.
- Add cabbage and stir for approximately 1 minute.
- Add vinegar, salt, bay leaves, clove-studded onion and enough water to keep the cabbage from burning.
- Cover and simmer for 45 minutes, adding water only as needed.
- At the last minute, add wine and bring to a quick boil.
- Remove bay leaves and studded onion before serving.

Celebrating Light

The Jewish community has been part of our city since the first Jews arrived as goldminers in the 1860s. In fact, Victoria was the site of British North America's first synagogue in built west of Toronto, and many non-Jews contributed to the building fund. A description of the laying of the cornerstone in 1863 shows the multicultural mix of Victoria at the time. "Prayers were read by a Christian clergyman, Chief Justice Cameron pronounced the benediction, the German Sing Verein, the French benevolent society, St. Andrews Society and Masonic Lodge all participated, and the band from HMS *Topaz* at Esquimalt played for the occasion."

POTATO LATKES

The Jewish festival we have been most often invited to share is Hanukkah, symbolized by the burning of the Menorah candles. Just the mention of Hanukkah makes our taste buds drool, as our friends always serve latkes, those lacy little potato pancakes served with sour cream or applesauce. Here's the recipe.
Serves 6.

4 medium potatoes
1 onion
2 eggs, beaten
1 tsp salt
⅛ tsp pepper
3 Tbsp flour
½ cup oil

- Peel and grate the potatoes.
- Peel and finely chop or grate the onion, combine with potatoes.
- Stir in beaten egg. Add salt, pepper and enough of the flour to bind and thicken.
- Heat 2 tablespoons of the oil in a frying pan. Drop in 2 or 3 tablespoons of the mixture to make small latkes. Fry until brown and crisp, turning once.
- Serve on a heated platter with bowls of sour cream and applesauce.

Sushi and Shrines

Victoria is noted for its Japanese restaurants. There are several of them, ranging from a takeout sushi kiosk in Hillside Mall to restaurants offering full-scale sushi bars, private tatami rooms or communal seating around a large hot plate where the chef juggles cleavers and pepper grinders while cooking Japanese-style steak. This is the familiar face of Victoria's Japanese community, most of whom have settled here since the 1950s. A visit to the Shinto shrine on the grounds of the Art Gallery of Greater Victoria shows another aspect, the closely related religious and artistic face of the culture. It is serene and beautiful and the only Shinto shrine in North America. This is our favourite hidden corner of Victoria, a place to catch our breath when the pace of life gets too fast. If you would like to try a taste of Japan for yourself, visit Victoria Fujiya, a little grocery on Shelbourne Street where you can purchase everything from dried nori (seaweed used in rice rolls) to jars of delicious pickled ginger and the incredible hot horseradish paste called wasabi. Bottles of sake – Japanese rice wine – can be obtained in any liquor store. Serve it warmed.

SAKE STEAMED CHICKEN

This is traditionally served as part of a picnic, with the delicate slices beautifully arranged in the bento boxes. It can also be served as an hors d'oeuvre. Ideally it is made with duck, but it's hard to buy duck breasts.

Makes 24 slices, enough to serve 6 as part of an hors d'oeuvre selection.

2 whole chicken breasts, boned but with skin left on
1 tsp salt
1 Tbsp sake

- Place both boned chicken breasts skin side up on a small oven-proof plate and sprinkle with teaspoon of salt. Cover with plastic wrap, refrigerate and let marinate for at least 3 hours.
- Set up an Oriental steamer over a pan of boiling water.
- Remove chicken from fridge, remove plastic, add the sake and steam for 7 minutes.
- While chicken is steaming, preheat a broiler on highest setting.
- Remove platter of chicken from the steamer and slide under the broiler about 3 inches from heat. Broil for approximately 2 minutes or until the skin is a rich golden brown.
- Cool to room temperature, then carve into ¼ inch slices.

A Taste of India

There are several Indian restaurants in Victoria reflecting the small but active East Indian community here. Like all restaurants, some come and go, but the one we have enjoyed consistently for many years is the Taj Mahal on Herald Street. Like many East Indian business ventures, this started as a family-run operation reflecting the cultural values of its owners. Ingredients for Indian cooking can be purchased at B & V Market on Quadra Street, a little shop that has also been in operation for over twenty years. It's opposite the Italian Bakery. What a great multicultural shopping stop!

VEGETABLE BIRYANI

This dish makes a large amount and is a vegetarian meal in itself when served with plain yogurt, or can feed double the amount of people as a rice dish accompanying the ground lamb curry on page 71.

Serves 6 to 8 as a complete meal.

1 cup eggplant, cubed
1 cup carrots, cubed
1 cup peas, freshly shelled
1 cup cauliflower buds
1 onion, chopped
1 garlic clove, chopped
1 large tomato, chopped
1 green pepper, chopped
2 Tbsp butter
4 whole cloves
4 cardamom pods
1 cinnamon stick, 2 inches long
2 cups white rice, uncooked
½ tsp cayenne pepper
2 tsp salt
4 cups water

- Chop or dice all the vegetables.
- In a large Dutch oven melt the butter, add the garlic, onion and green pepper and stir for 2 minutes.
- Add the whole cloves, cardamom pods and broken cinnamon

stick. Continue to stir until the onion begins to brown.

- Add the tomato and cook, stirring, for approximately 7 minutes or until the tomato breaks down to form a smooth sauce.
- Add the rice, cayenne and salt, and sauté until the rice becomes coated with the tomato mixture.
- Add all the vegetables and stir until they are coated.
- Add the water, reduce heat, cover and let simmer for 20 minutes or until all the water has been absorbed. By this time the rice and vegetables will be steamed and tender.
- Serve heaped in a large bowl, accompanied by plain yogurt.

stuffed primrose avocado, cheeses decorated with edible flowers and herbs

Several generations sitting down to Christmas dinner at the Helmckens

11

City of Gardens

We couldn't finish this book without dealing with the current, rather delightful, concept of Victoria as "the garden city." Not only is it true, but the length of the growing season means some edible flowers are available in the gardens year round and we have become avid users.

Victoria gives an overwhelming summer impression of flowers, flowers, and more flowers. They burgeon forth from over eight hundred hanging baskets in the downtown core, make geometric splashes of colour in formal parks, and blossom in profusion in private gardens and wild areas of the city, making a feast for the senses.

Stroll through the Rockland area and feast your eyes on the formal landscaping around elegant homes. Visit the public gardens of the Lieutenant Governor's residence on Rockland Avenue, and soak in the scent of the roses. Dawdle around historic James Bay and enjoy the older houses garnished with "gingerbread" ornamentation, surrounded by an unruly cottage-garden riot of flowers. Many of these flowers are edible.

Don't stop there. Visit the natural outcrops on Beacon Hill and Gonzales Hill, the Gorge walks and the Swan Lake Nature Sanctuary, and revel in the sight and smells of wildflowers, for even within the city limits, wildflowers are prolific. Drifts of bluebells and primroses are followed by carpets of daisies and buttercups, and a multitude of other herbs and flowers. And flowers here are not restricted to spring and summer. Fall is the time for vivid and surprising patches of purple from the autumn crocuses — known as "Naked Ladies" because their blooms appear without surrounding foliage. Though not harvested here, this is the crocus whose stamens, when dried, become the expensive spice saffron.

Winter, too, has its flowering beauties. Our mild climate nurtures the gentle glow of winter-blooming jasmine, and late-blooming heaths and heathers and winter pansies. When the rest of Canada lies in a snowy deep freeze, we rejoice at the sight of snowdrops and spring crocuses, often as early as January or February. For seventeen years, the Victoria Chamber of Commerce has taken wicked delight in organizing the annual blossom count — in late February! — and sending the result, with an accompanying bowl of spring flowers, to the weather persons at TV stations across the country . . . . How nasty can you get?

Victoria gardens are a wonderful source of flowery ingredients for summer dishes. Cooking with flowers adds a whole new dimension to a special occasion. Imagine an afternoon tea with flower petal butters, or a special dinner party with the scent of flowers not only drifting in from the garden, but subtly stirring the senses by rising from the plate before you. Next time you need a special cake, forget the worries of elaborate decorative icing; use plain icing and add a wreath of fragrant edible flowers and herbs. Andrea did this for a wedding cake and it received rave reviews. Flowers are a quick and easy way to decorate. They impress your guests, and save you time and anxiety.

SENSIBLE RULES WHEN COOKING WITH FLOWERS

1) If you cannot positively identify the flower, don't use it.
2) Use only flowers from your own garden to ensure they haven't been sprayed with chemicals.
3) Check that there are no little insects hiding among the leaves or petals; you don't want unwelcome visitors on your guest's plate.
4) Please don't pick wildflowers in parks or natural areas. They are there for everyone to enjoy.

ROSE PETAL "HONEY"

The fragrant rose is often the flower of choice for a cook's first foray into edible flora. This easy recipe for Rose Petal "Honey" makes a wonderful and imaginative gift from the garden city.

24 fragrant rose blossoms
32 red clover blossoms
82 white clover blossoms
10 lbs sugar
1 strawberry
   or 2 cranberries
6 cups water
1 Tbsp alum*

- Boil the flowers, strawberry and water for 10 minutes. Strain and keep liquid.
- Add the sugar. Bring to the boil again and cook for 12 minutes. Stir in alum.
- Pour into sterilized jelly jars and cap with self-sealing lids.
- Use this "honey" as a topping on pastries or ice cream, as a fruit tart glaze, or drizzle over fresh fruit.

* *Alum can be purchased from drugstores*

ALMOST INSTANT FLOWER POWER

- *Add a large handful of lemon balm leaves to a jug of lemonade and garnish with a few blue borage blossoms.*
- *Add showy nasturtium blossoms to a green salad. The whole flower can be eaten. It has a slightly peppery taste with a hint of sweetness from the nectar hidden in the cone.*
- *Add mint leaves and flowers to the slices of lemon in the ice water jug.*
- *Float rose petals in finger bowls. Use when serving crab.*
- *Sprinkle calendula petals and chopped parsley on top of a cream soup — use only the calendula marigold, not the African marigold (Tagetes).*
- *For a stunning variation of Victoria sponge cake (see recipe on page 78), sandwich the layers with rose petal or rose hip*

jelly instead of strawberry jam. Swirl whipped cream on top. Add a wreath of variegated mint leaves and small rosebuds or individual rose petals.

- *Make flower butters by pressing pungent flower petals such as honeysuckle, clove carnation or rose all around a ½-cup pat of unsalted butter. Wrap with cling film and leave for a day or two in the fridge to allow the flavours to penetrate. Unwrap, leaving the petals in place, and bring up to room temperature before serving.*

Getting Hip

The wild roses in the hedgerows and bramble patches are reputed to produce better hips than cultivated roses. The hips are not only prized for their flavour, but contain a high concentration of vitamin C. The Coast Salish people pounded the hips and mixed them into jerky. Pioneer families fed their children spoonfuls of rosehip syrup to ward off colds. Apparently the favoured time to collect the hips was after the first cold period. Folklore says a cold snap "sets" the goodness inside.

ROSE HIP JELLY

We savour this unusual flavour mid-winter – a taste of summer in the midst of the February rains.

2 lbs rose hips
5 cups water
2 cups sugar (approximately)
3 Tbsp lemon juice

- Wash and drain rose hips. Chop coarsely in food processor.
- Combine with water and boil for 1 hour or until soft.
- Place in jelly bag and leave to drip overnight.
- Measure the juice. For every 2½ cups of juice add 2 cups of sugar.
- Heat slowly until all the sugar is dissolved, then bring to a full boil. Boil steadily until setting point is reached (about 20 to 30 minutes, but keep testing by dropping a little on a cool saucer to see if it sets).
- Skim off the surface scum and stir in lemon juice to taste.
- Pour into sterilized jelly jars and seal.

Floral Vinegars

One of the easiest ways to explore the flavours of flowers is to make floral vinegars. They add a unique taste to homemade salad dressing. Red nasturtiums make a beautiful pale orange vinegar; blackberries a dark purple vinegar; mints a pale green one. We've even used grated ginger root; it's a little cloudy but the flavour is good. The blackberry vinegar is the one we use most often with wild salad ingredients.

ELDER FLOWER VINEGAR

This is the basic method that can be used with any pungent edible flower or herb.

Elder flowers
white wine vinegar

- Pack a wide-mouthed jar full of elder flowers.
- Pour in white wine vinegar to fill it completely.
- Screw on the lid and stand in a dark place for 2 to 3 weeks.
- Strain into a regular bottle and use in salad dressings.

Proportions for Homemade Salad Dressing
1 part flower- or herb-flavoured vinegar
2 parts good-quality oil
herbs to taste

- Place ingredients in a screw-top jar and shake vigorously.

~~~

Floral Luncheon

For a very special Victoria finale, we present a floral luncheon for four people that is a feast for all the senses. It is easy to host, as the appetizer and dessert are prepared ahead, and the entrée quickly stir-fried just before serving. Serve inside or out on a beautifully set table with a centrepiece of roses, accompanied by a delicately dry white wine such as a Niersteiner.

STUFFED PRIMROSE AVOCADO

Traditionally, primrose blossoms were used to add colour to the shells of hard-boiled eggs at Eastertime. In this recipe they add not only colour, but a delicate taste to a spring appetizer. Prepare this recipe just before the guests come and add the primroses at the last minute. If primrose season is over, substitute small yellow pansies.
Serves 4.

2 avocados
2 cups fresh crabmeat
3 to 4 Tbsp any creamy salad dressing
4 thin wedges of fresh pear
4 thin wedges of fresh peach
1 Tbsp freshly picked primroses

- Halve the avocados and remove stones.
- Mix crabmeat with the creamy dressing and fill the 4 avocado halves.
- Tuck a slice of peach and a slice of pear into each mound of crab. (Can be refrigerated at this point for up to an hour.)
- Stud the crab mixture with primroses and serve immediately as an appetizer.
- Can be accompanied with tiny fingers of hot buttered toast.

STIR-FRIED PRAWNS WITH CHRYSANTHEMUMS AND CARNATIONS

The delicate flavours of most flower petals are lost when cooked, which is why they are usually used as garnish. An exception is the hardy chrysanthemum, which can actually be used during the stir-fry process without killing the flavour. This is a spectacular-looking entrée that everyone wants to photograph. Cook the noodles first and keep warm; stir-fry the preassembled ingredients at the last minute.
Serves 4.

1 lb Chinese egg noodles
2 Tbsp sunflower oil
6 spring onions, diagonally sliced
3 garlic cloves, chopped
1 inch ginger root, grated
1½ lbs large fresh prawns, peeled
petals from 1 large head of white chrysanthemum
1 to 2 Tbsp light soy sauce
½ fresh lime
petals from 1 large red carnation

- Cook the noodles in a large pot of boiling, salted water for 3 to 4 minutes. Drain and keep warm in a large serving dish.
- Heat oil in wok until almost smoking. Add garlic, onions and ginger and stir well for 30 seconds or until onions are soft.
- Add the prawns and chrysanthemum petals and stir-fry for 2 minutes or until the prawns are pink.
- Add soy sauce to taste and the lime juice. Stir-fry for 10 seconds.
- Pour over the noodles and sprinkle red carnation petals on top. Serve immediately.

~~~

Floral Ice Cream

The finishing touch to a floral luncheon is a homemade floral ice cream. The only problem is that once you start making homemade ice cream, you may never want to taste the store-bought variety again. There are several specialty kitchen shops in Victoria that carry ice cream makers, ranging from inexpensive hand-cranked ones to top-of-the-line electric models. For an occasional treat, the hand-cranked one with the liner that is kept chilled in the freezer works just fine.

WAR FOR A PIECE

Wars have been fought over pieces of land marked by the deep blue patches of wild camas lily seen in the natural areas of Beacon Hill Park – the edible bulb was once so prized by the First Nations people that they fought to keep its habitat in their territory. Camas provided much of the starch in the Indian diet. The bulbs were dug in the spring. Fires were lit in pits lined with stones, and then the fire was raked out and the bulbs were placed in the pit on green leaves and left to steam. Early settlers ate camas pie, but the modern settler should not be tempted to try eating one – it is almost impossible to distinguish the bulb of the camas lily from the similar death camas lily, which is deadly poison. Besides, thanks to the sprawl of the city, the camas lily is now much less common and deserves protection.

JASMINE ICE CREAM

For those of you without an ice cream maker, this recipe gives directions for freezing in the icebox of a fridge. The fridge method does work, but the texture is not great because of the water content, which produces more of a grainy sherbet than a true ice cream. We suggest you try and borrow an ice cream maker. Then the results jump from "very nice" to "magnificent." This recipe can also be made with rose petals. Substitute rose water for the lemon juice.
Serves 4.

3 Tbsp fresh jasmine flowers
½ cup boiling water
½ cup berry sugar, or run granulated sugar in the blender
    for a few seconds
½ lemon, squeeze for juice
1¼ cups whipping cream
1 drop yellow food colouring (optional)
extra handful jasmine flowers, for decoration

- Pour the boiling water over half of the jasmine flowers and let stand for 1 hour.
- Gradually bring the water and flowers to the boil again while stirring in the sugar. Boil until syrupy.
- Strain and pour syrup into food processor. Add remaining flowers and liquidize.

- Cool, then stir in lemon juice.
- Add the cream while whisking lightly. (Add optional drop of yellow food colouring at this point.)
- If you have an ice cream freezer, use following manufacturer's instructions.
- To freeze in a fridge, pour mixture into ice tray and freeze until edges are just firm.
- Transfer to a bowl, beat thoroughly and refreeze in ice tray. (You may wish to repeat these last two steps to get a good consistency.)
- Transfer ice cream from freezer to fridge ½ hour before serving.
- Serve with lots of fresh jasmine sprinkled on top.

Bon Appétit!

Index

Andrea and David Spalding are freelance writers and heritage consultants who live on Pender Island, B.C., where, among many other pursuits, they operate the Arbutus Retreat Bed and Breakfast, known for its gourmet breakfasts. Andrea has worked in several food related businesses and is the family "ritual master" for all important occasions. David has a long-standing interest in consuming foods and pursues unusual avenues of historical and scientific research.

Both have many writing credits. Andrea co-authored *The Pender Palate* (Loon Books, 1992) and has several successful children's books published. Andrea is a member of ACTRA and is a well-known storyteller, giving workshops and doing television programs. She has written over a hundred scripts and, in 1980, her historical play, "One-Way Ticket," won her an Alberta Culture teleplay award and an ACTRA nomination. David's most recent book is *Dinosaur Hunters, 150 Years of Extraordinary Discoveries* (Key Porter, 1993). He is an active member of many museum associations and paleontological societies.